IF YOU DON'T *FIGHT* THEN YOU DON'T *WIN*

BECOMING GREAT. ONE BATTLE AT A TIME.

HOPE CARPENTER

AVAIL

OTHER BOOKS BY HOPE CARPENTER

The Most Beautiful Disaster:
How God Makes Miracles Out of Our Mistakes

WHAT PEOPLE ARE SAYING ABOUT *IF YOU DON'T FIGHT, THEN YOU DON'T WIN*

If You Don't Fight, Then You Won't Win will inspire, equip, and empower you to realize your potential and step into your God-given purpose. In her much loved, down-to-earth, no-nonsense way, Hope shows us that with God all things are possible.

—Christine Caine
Founder, A21 and Propel Women

You will be amazed by the practical insights, wit, and wisdom that Hope Carpenter shares in her new book *If You Don't Fight, Then You Don't Win*. Her transparency in sharing how God helped her overcome painful life experiences has positioned her to coach and mentor others worldwide to win in the battles of life. You will find Hope's book to be passionate, compelling, challenging, and equalizing. I highly recommend it!

—Lisa Osteen Comes
Author, *It's On The Way*
Associate Pastor, Lakewood Church

This work is more than a book, it's a blueprint to an overcoming kind of life. In this amazing work, Hope masterfully lays out the truth that we can overcome, outlast, and endure whatever adversity we encounter. She reveals strategies and secrets to overcome fickle feelings, perform under pressure, and experience life as God intended. Read this book at your own risk; it will convince you of the biblical truth that if you don't fight, then you don't win.

—Dharius Daniels
Author of *Relational Intelligence*
Pastor, Change Church

Calvin Coolidge, the 30th President of the United States, said, "Nothing in this world can take the place of persistence. Talent will not: nothing is more common than unsuccessful men with talent. Genius will not; unrewarded genius is almost a proverb. Education will not: the world is full of educated derelicts. Persistence and determination alone are omnipotent." One of the most important lessons my pastor, Dr. Lester Sumrall, reinforced in my life was this: "I did not quit." Those who contend in the arena of conflict will certainly become the recipients of life's hard knocks, as well as our adversary's fiery missiles. The difference between success and failure is this—champions get up one more time.

My dear friend, Hope Carpenter understands this! Her understanding is not the result of reading about someone else's victories—but rather, from her own experience in the inevitable conflicts that occur in ministry and in life. In her new book, *If You Don't Fight, Then You Don't Win*, she makes the case for persistence and determination to become successful in any endeavor. She knows what all believers must know—if you don't fight, then you don't win. However, when you do fight—and keep on fighting—you never lose, and total victory is your reward. Fight on!

—Dr. Rod Parsley
Pastor and Founder, World Harvest Church
Columbus, Ohio

I am so happy Hope wrote this book. "IF YOU DON'T FIGHT YOU DON'T WIN!"

Too often, we overcomplicate things like hearing God's voice and being led by Him, leaving us confused and doubting instead of moving forward into all that He has for us. In this practical guidebook, Hope gives us the tools we need to discern the voice of God so we can walk in an even deeper relationship with Him.
—Real Talk Kim

Hope Carpenter writes heartfelt, honest books that bring life change. She doesn't hold back and challenges readers to be everything they're destined to be in her new book *If You Don't Fight Then You Don't Win*! Challenging, but so uplifting!

—Chandler Bolt
CEO of selfpublishing.com

Giving up, not trying, and longing for easier comes naturally—without trying. Hope Carpenter knows and acknowledges that and still reminds us that *If You Don't Fight, Then You Don't Win*. This is more than a self-help motivational book. It is Hope Carpenter personifying her name, Hope. Fight and Win.

—Sam Chand
Leadership Consultant
Author of *Leadership Pain*

Life is replete with pain, tragedy, and long walks through the wilderness. In *If You Don't Fight, Then You Don't Win*, Hope Carpenter makes a compelling case that the quality of your journey through the valley of the shadow of death and who you become on the other side depends on how much you are willing to fight for it!

—Martijn van Tilborgh
Co-Founder and Co-Owner of AVAIL
Founder of Four Rivers Media

Copyright © 2024 by Hope Carpenter

Published by AVAIL

All rights reserved. No portion of this book may be reproduced, stored in a retrieval system, or transmitted in any form or by any means—electronic, mechanical, photocopy, recording, scanning, or other—except for brief quotations in critical reviews or articles, without prior written permission of the author.

Unless otherwise noted, Scripture quotations are taken from the Holy Bible, New International Version®, NIV®. Copyright © 1973, 1978, 1984, 2011 by Biblica, Inc.™ Used by permission of Zondervan. All rights reserved worldwide. www.zondervan.com. The "NIV" and "New International Version" are trademarks registered in the United States Patent and Trademark Office by Biblica, Inc.™ | Scripture quotations marked AMP are taken from the Amplified® Bible (AMP), Copyright © 2015 by The Lockman Foundation. Used by permission. www.lockman.org | Scripture quotations marked GNT are from the Good News Translation in Today's English Version- Second Edition Copyright © 1992 by American Bible Society. Used by Permission. | Scripture quotations marked KJV are taken from the King James Version of the Bible. Public domain. | Scripture quotations Scripture quotations marked NAB are taken from the New American Bible, revised edition © 2010, 1991, 1986, 1970 Confraternity of Christian Doctrine, Washington, D.C. and are used by permission of the copyright owner. All Rights Reserved. No part of the New American Bible may be reproduced in any form without permission in writing from the copyright owner. |Scripture quotations marked NASB are taken from the (NASB®) New American Standard Bible®, Copyright © 1960, 1971, 1977, 1995, 2020 by The Lockman Foundation. Used by permission. All rights reserved. www.lockman.org | Scripture quotations marked NLT are taken from the Holy Bible, New Living Translation, copyright © 1996, 2004, 2015 by Tyndale House Foundation. Used by permission of Tyndale House Publishers, Inc., Carol Stream, Illinois 60188. All rights reserved. | Scripture quotations marked NLV are taken from the Holy Bible, New Life Version, copyright © 1969, 2003 by Barbour Publishing, Inc. | The ESV® Bible (The Holy Bible, English Standard Version®). ESV® Text Edition: 2016. Copyright © 2001 by Crossway, a publishing ministry of Good News Publishers. The ESV® text has been reproduced in cooperation with and by permission of Good News Publishers. Unauthorized reproduction of this publication is prohibited. All rights reserved. | Scripture quotations marked NKJV are taken from the New King James Version®. Copyright © 1982 by Thomas Nelson. Used by permission. All rights reserved.

For foreign and subsidiary rights, contact the author.

Cover design by Sara Young
Cover photo by Andrew van Tilborgh

ISBN: 978-1-960678-75-1   1 2 3 4 5 6 7 8 9 10

Printed in the United States of America

This book is dedicated to every person who feels like giving up, throwing in the towel. For the single moms who have been giving it their all—working two or three jobs just to pay the bills—but don't have time to take the kids to the park or to get ice cream. For the addict who works so hard to stay clean, landed a good job, but woke up in a crack house after he swore he'd never do it again. This book is for the people who don't feel good enough, smart enough, or brave enough to even try one more time to do something significant in life. For the tired people. For the abused people. The broke people. The handicapped people. The wrong-side-of-the-tracks people. This book is for me. This book is for you.

Every human alive has a list of why he or she feels they just can't "do it" anymore. They have a flawed belief system that says the good life isn't for them. I dedicate this book to you because you will find that you do have the potential to rise from whatever desperate situation you are in if you will muster up enough strength, faith, and courage to fight for what is yours. I believe in you, and more importantly . . . God believes in you.

CONTENTS

Introduction 11

CHAPTER 1. **We Weren't Promised "Easy"**......... 17

CHAPTER 2. **Fickle Feelings**..................... 31

CHAPTER 3. **We Have an Enemy—Be Aware**..... 43

CHAPTER 4. **Pressure Produces if You Let It**...... 59

CHAPTER 5. **Divinely Molded** 77

CHAPTER 6. **Trouble's Knocking** 89

CHAPTER 7. **How's Your Heart?** 109

CHAPTER 8. **Fight the Good Fight of Faith**....... 123

CHAPTER 9. **What's Stopping You?** 135

CHAPTER 10. **We Win** 145

INTRODUCTION

I used to think that the rich people and the famous people—those at the top of the food chain, so to speak—just were the "lucky ones." Maybe they were born with a silver spoon in their mouths or just got a lucky break. Maybe they were born smarter or on the right side of the tracks. Now that I've lived fifty-five years, I've come to realize that none of that was true. Yes, there are instances when the boss of an organization does have wealthy parents or the high-paid executive does have a high IQ, but for the most part, those are not the determining factors of their success.

The truth is, we don't want to admit that we have the same twenty-four hours in a day or that we're simply not motivated enough to do the necessary things that help us to live a better life than we're living right now. We really do want to win the lottery and never have to work again. We desire for one of our reels to go viral, so we can get paid mega money, sit back, and let the checks roll in. We are not naturally inclined to want to get up and grind to make things happen in our lives.

> We are not naturally inclined to want to get up and grind to make things happen in our lives.

I don't think it's always been that way because many years ago (none that we remember) if you wanted to eat, you had to hunt for it or plant it. If you wanted a new dress, you had to make it yourself. Long gone are the days of burning the candle to read and then making another candle when that one burned out. We have instant coffee, oatmeal, and grits (if you're in the South). We eat microwave dinners. We're insta-famous (for what, I don't know). We give our kids money for doing absolutely nothing—except being cute. Oh, I forgot to mention my absolute favorites: DoorDash and Instacart! I mean, who can live without them?

Don't get me wrong. I'm thankful for all of the modern luxuries of life, but I'm afraid we have been luxury-ed into becoming a weak society where having to work hard, grind, persevere, believe God for, and pray until something happens is a foreign concept. We give up way too early. We move on to the next husband or wife because we don't "feel" in love anymore.

HOPE CARPENTER

We stop going to church because someone didn't speak to us. We stop tithing: "This must not work. After all, I gave my 10 percent two weeks in a row, and the Lord hasn't blessed me financially yet!" We go to the gym for a few weeks and never go back because we only lost two pounds. We give up way too soon, and the truth is, some things just take time. We are an instant-gratification society, and we just don't know how to wait or fight for what we want.

My husband is the most disciplined human I know. I always say that when I grow up, I want to be just like him. I met Ron in 1987, and from that day until now, he has always gone to the gym four to five days a week. That in itself is commendable, but here's the best part: it doesn't matter if he's sick, running late, out of town, in a hotel, or has to get up early. It doesn't matter the situation: HE IS GOING TO GO TO THE GYM. That, my friend, is what I'm talking about. Sheer determination and grit. Those are the qualities that separate the winners from the losers. It's not the amount of money in your bank account or what side of the tracks that you came from. It's the mindset that, *If I don't fight, then I don't win.*

I've been around now for fifty-five years, and I feel like I've just started living and walking out my full potential. I had a lot to overcome, healing to do, and severe amounts of cleanup after the crash and burn of my fragile attempt to "do life". I see so many people stuck, going in circles, settling for way less than they were created for and I feel like I'm qualified to help navigate and steer those who find themselves where I was so that they

IF YOU DON'T *FIGHT,* THEN YOU DON'T *WIN*

can find their way and start running in the right direction. I see young moms trying to navigate running a home, getting kids to daycare on time and hopefully loading the dishwasher before the ants arrive. I see young husbands trying to be the priests of their homes who barely know three scriptures and still long to meet up with their "homies" on the weekend to chill and watch the games while their wives and kids desperately need their husbands and dad at home to help with chores and just throw the ball in the backyard. People who have no clue how to run their races well and seem to end up in mess after mess, on a never-ending cycle of misery. It doesn't have to be this way. God did not bleed and die for us to merely *get by* by the skin of our teeth. His plans for us are good plans, to give us a great future that we gaze toward with hope.

Anything significant that happens in our lives is going to take time. Healing from trauma, gaining wealth, rebuilding trust, establishing a career, getting out of debt, starting over after a divorce, whatever it is. And I've also learned that God's timing and my timing are very different; I want what I want, and I want it now. But I've found that anything I desire or pursue is going to take longer than I want it to take. If I submit to God's process, it will be better than I could ever imagine.

Where are you in your life right now? Do you hate where you are? Do you think, *That only happens for* other people? Well, if that's you, then you're believing a lie. You're in the middle of the arena of life, your opponent is throwing haymakers, and you're about to go down for the count. What are you going to do? You can hit back a time or two, but that doesn't win the fight. You can even win a round or two and still lose. You've got to fight and keep fighting until you're the last man standing. You might be bruised and have teeth knocked out and blood in your eyes, but you won!

I'm your trainer. I'm in your corner, yelling for you to keep swinging. You might be lying on the mat, thinking it's over, but I'm over here screaming, "Get up. You've got this. You're stronger than you think you are!" because if you don't fight, then you don't win. And I know you're a winner. How? Because God created you to win, to do great things, and to live a wonderful life. That's why so many of us are unfulfilled and dissatisfied. We aren't living up to our God-given potential.

> **God created you to win, to do great things, and to live a wonderful life. That's why so many of us are unfulfilled and dissatisfied. We aren't living up to our God-given potential.**

There is a life out there that is amazing, abundant, and fulfilling—that will give you a hope and a future to be excited about—but YOU have got to fight for it. Put on your boxing gloves, and get ready for the fight of your life.

WE WEREN'T PROMISED "EASY"

*"When you catch a glimpse of your potential,
that's when passion is born."*
—ZIG ZIGLAR

*"Never underestimate the power of dreams and the
influence of the human spirit. We are all the same in this
notion: The potential for greatness lives within each of us."*
—WILMA RUDOLPH[1]

---

1 "The Official Website of Wilma Rudolph," *Wilma Rudolph*, 16 May 2022, wilmarudolph.com/.

IF YOU DON'T *FIGHT,* THEN YOU DON'T *WIN*

God has done mind-blowing things in the life of this little girl from the metropolis of Calhoun Falls, South Carolina, population one thousand—provided no one's on vacation. There were only sixty-four kids in my graduating class. And the only intersection in town had a flashing light. It never turned red or green; it only blinked yellow. My parents worked in the local cotton mill where my dad was an electrician and my mom an office supervisor. I grew up in the Southern Baptist church until I was twelve years old. At that time, we made a major church shift to the Pentecostal Holiness Church where we clapped our hands and—can you believe it—raised our hands during worship! I felt like I had died and gone to Heaven.

My spiritual life radically shifted when we changed churches. I was on fire for God, even at such a young age and knew that I wanted to serve the Lord whole-heartedly. The funny thing is ... I always knew, deep down inside, that my life was created for so much more than what I saw around me. I knew that God had created me to do big things—big things for HIM—not to further my own agenda or for my name's sake but for His name's sake. I had no idea what that looked like or even how to get "there," but I knew that I wanted to fulfill the purpose of God for my life. So, I got up, got on the train, and went for it.

> I knew that I wanted to fulfill the purpose of God for my life. So, I got up, got on the train, and went for it.

Here I am, fifty-five years old, and God continuously blows my mind. I know that I'm not smart enough, popular enough, rich enough, educated enough, savvy enough, beautiful enough, or from the right-side-of-town-enough to be where I am today. Have I arrived? Certainly not. Have other people done more, achieved more, made more money, and acquired more followers than me? Absolutely, but I know that I haven't even really started to become everything that God has ordained for me.

I married my college sweetheart, Ron Carpenter, and we started out on our journey in 1990, wanting to save the world. We had no money, social media, cell phone, Siri, or Bible Hub. We got "leads" for prospective church members by people writing down their names, numbers, and addresses on napkins or bank deposit slips. We then used our handy-dandy map to

HOPE CARPENTER

find their homes and went to meet them one by one. During this time, I worked three jobs so that Ron could focus on trying to grow this church of three members: Ron, our song leader, and me. We met in an old warehouse with loading docks in the back that we covered with green plastic shower curtains. (They were supposed to look like green curtains.) We had an old upright piano and a microphone from Radio Shack, and off we went—Redemption Outreach Center, August 1991.

Thinking back to our early days, I wonder, *Why did anyone even stay?* IT WAS BAD.

Our metal building had no air conditioning in South Carolina in August—not exactly a recipe for success. Ron would play the drums and then take the mic to do all the other platform stuff and preach. I would play the piano and then leave after worship to teach children's church for two or three kids. After church, we would gather up all the nursery toys and take them home to disinfect and clean them, and Ron would lay his head in my lap and cry because we knew how awful it was. But here's the secret sauce. Are you ready? Are you sure? WE DIDN'T QUIT! We continued to plow away with the burning desire and vision that God had given us for a radical, multicultural congregation in the deep South, even when the odds were stacked against us.

Ron and I did a lot wrong. I could write another book on what *not* to do in church planting—money handling, pastoring, leading people, hiring, firing, marriage, and child-rearing—we did so many things wrong. We had children with no health insurance. We had no mentors to help us navigate contracts and business plans. We had grown up in legalism, which didn't allow us to admit sin or struggle and threw us into a performance-based lifestyle that ultimately led to an emotional breakdown for me at thirty-five years old. Add to that nine years of a double life during which I was unfaithful to my husband and, ultimately, almost lost my marriage. We struggled for so long, but I'm not going to focus on all the wrong we did. Just know that we did it. My part is chronicled in my book *The Most Beautiful Disaster*.

> **What I am going to talk about in this book is the one thing we did right. We never gave up!**

What I am going to talk about in this book is the one thing we did right. We never gave up! Every time we failed in any area we would cry, curse, drink some (gasp—shameful!), and sin a few times. But then we would always come back to our center—our core truth—and that was the fact that we loved God with all of our hearts, and we loved His people—the church and the not-churched. No matter what, we continued to let the purpose of God push us toward our destiny.

HOPE CARPENTER

Nowhere in scripture does it say that trials, trouble, heartache, setbacks, and devastation won't be part of our stories. As a matter of fact, it tells us that all of those things are a part of living in this world. John 16:33 says, "I have told you these things, so that in me you may have peace. In this world you will have trouble. But take heart! I have overcome the world." This one Scripture tells us that although all the yucky stuff is inevitable, it's a fixed fight. You have to fight, though, nonetheless.

Another valuable concept to learn as a Christian leader is this: just because you are saved, you are not perfect, nor are you expected to be. Proverbs 24:16 says, "For though the righteous fall seven times, they rise again, but the wicked stumble when calamity strikes." Perfection is not our goal as Christians in business, ministry, or life—but getting back up again should be our response every single time. I truly believe this is the unmistakable difference between people who know the Lord and those who don't. We have the ability to rise again while the wicked stumble and never recover.

It's not surprising that my favorite person in the Bible is Joseph. I feel like I have lived his life in so many areas. While he is mentioned earlier, his story really starts in Genesis 37. He couldn't help that he was favored by his father, that he wore that "special coat," and that he was the love child of his parents, Jacob and Rachel. His brothers, however, were jealous of him. They knew of their father's great love for Joseph and decided to get rid of him by staging his death and blaming it on a bear. They threw him into a deep, dark pit where he screamed for

IF YOU DON'T *FIGHT,* THEN YOU DON'T *WIN*

help as his brothers listened and did nothing. Eventually, his brothers sold him to some passing merchants who took him to Egypt to be a slave.

Joseph was sold to a man by the name of Potiphar who served as captain of Pharaoh's guard. He must have been so hurt and angry with his brothers and confused as to why God had allowed all of this pain. Nonetheless, Joseph worked hard, proved himself trustworthy, and eventually became the chief servant in Potiphar's house. He wasn't home free, however. Potiphar's wife plotted and schemed to seduce him. When he denied her, she accused him of raping her. Yet another lie . . . another betrayal. This time, Joseph was thrown into prison where he proved faithful yet again. He refused to allow the circumstances that he found himself in to define him. Joseph chose to rise above them every single time. Joseph is my hero!

While Joseph was imprisoned, he spent his time using his gift of interpreting dreams. He didn't sit in a corner sucking his thumb, boiling with anger, cursing his brothers, or backsliding and letting everyone have it on Facebook. No! He prospered in every situation he found himself in. Joseph certainly didn't deserve any of this, but here's the clincher: the good, the bad, and the ugly that happens in our lives are never wasted. God promises to use every single thing that we go through for our good and for His glory: "And we know that in all things God works for the good of those who love him, who have been called according to his purpose" (Romans 8:28).

HOPE CARPENTER

Genesis 50 explains why Joseph went through all of the pain and devastation. There was a famine in the land, and its effects stretched into Canaan where Joseph's father and brothers lived. They heard that there was food stored in Egypt, and Israel, Joseph's father, sent some of his sons to Egypt to buy food. Now, mind you, Joseph had pressed on, been faithful, and had been released from the Egyptian prison. He now had a family of his own and had risen to the position of vizier, which was basically a high-ranking advisor, and was second only to Pharaoh. And guess who was in charge of distributing all of the food during the famine? Yes, you guessed it. Joseph was. Isn't that how God tends to work?

So, Joseph came face-to-face with his brothers once again. He could have chosen to withhold the very thing they wanted and needed. He had the power, and he had the right. When their eyes met, Joseph's eyes filled with tears, and he said, "You intended to harm me, but God intended it all for good. He brought me to this position so that I could save the lives of many people" (Genesis 50:20, NLT). Joseph had been through so many difficulties, and trouble does something for you that nothing else can. He knew how faithful God had been to him through all of it, and he realized that God had placed him right there for that very purpose.

How many times have I looked up to Heaven, tears streaming down my face, and asked, "Why?" In my life, I have brought so much pain on myself, almost lost everything precious to me, and wondered if God could or would ever redeem my story, much less ever use me again. But just like in Joseph's life, nothing in our life is ever wasted. If we let Him, God can and will use all of our mistakes, junk, losses, heartaches, failures, and pain to refine, strengthen, and elevate us in a position so that redemption and restoration can happen through us. Joseph is my favorite person in the Bible because I can totally relate to his life. What God did for Joseph, He has done for me through all of my hurt, pain, trauma, and setbacks. And Genesis 50:20 is my favorite verse because I have watched God use every struggle that I have faced for my good and to help others rise from their own pit of depression, abuse, infidelity, low self-esteem, failure, and setback.

> **If we let Him, God can and will use all of our mistakes, junk, losses, heartaches, failures, and pain to refine, strengthen, and elevate us in a position so that redemption and restoration can happen through us.**

I don't know where you are today in this thing called life. You might be on top of the world and just wanted to read my latest book (Thank you!), but you might be at the point of giving up altogether. I feel like I need to remind you that as long as you've got a pulse, you have a purpose. Life is not over for you—no matter your age or condition—as long as there is breath in your lungs. Then again, you might not have lived long enough to have been faced with challenges and setbacks; just keep living. In every life some rain will fall but greater is He that is in you than anything that can come against you (my version of 1 John 4:4).

I think many of us live our lives with all of our God-given potential just lying dormant inside of us because we refuse to press on and fight for the life that we see in our mind and in our spirit. We've allowed pain, past hurts, and failures to derail us and hold us captive in a mediocre life that we hate. What if you fail? What if the business doesn't work out? What if no one bites? What if you lose the money? Let me ask you this—WHAT IF IT WORKS? If God has given you a dream, a vision, or even a word, it's not your responsibility to make it happen. It's God's responsibility to bring it to pass, and it's our responsibility to be faithful.

When the prophet Jeremiah was arguing with God over whether he was capable of fulfilling God's call on his life or not, Jeremiah 1:12 (NLT) tells us God's response: "I will certainly carry out all my plans." Jeremiah didn't have anything to worry about. We don't either. God will carry out the plans He has for our lives, but we have to be willing to get back up again after every disappointment, failure, heartbreak, and betrayal. We must trust God with our lives and believe that He will carry out HIS plans for OUR good and HIS glory.

IF YOU DON'T *FIGHT,* THEN YOU DON'T *WIN*

I don't want to spend my life just swinging and staying busy for the sake of "faithfulness." I want to swing and be focused and faithful in my lane, on my call, and in what I know that I am called to do. There will absolutely be obstacles because we have an enemy, the devil, who hates us. His very job description (see John 10:10) is to steal from us our dreams, our marriage, our happiness, our drive, our passion, and the good life that God has planned for us.

> **If God has given you a dream, a vision, or even a word, it's not your responsibility to make it happen. It's God's responsibility to bring it to pass, and it's our responsibility to be faithful.**

For years, I would get mad, frustrated, and knocked off my rocker when trials, trouble, and life happened to me. But when I grasped the revelation that trouble doesn't just hit some people but that it rains on the just and the unjust (see Matthew 5:45), it was a game changer for me. I realized that the enemy's job is to frustrate the heck out of me SO THAT I will quit—so that I will give up. This newfound knowledge made me furious that I had fallen for his tactics so many times, instead of squaring up my shoulders and giving it right back to him harder than he gave it to me.

The last part of John 10:10 (NAB, emphasis added) says, "I came so that they MIGHT have life and have it more abundantly." Whoa . . . might? More abundant than what? More abundant than the life you were living before you accepted Jesus as your savior. Your life should look better . . . different . . . more free, more alive . . . more abundant! So, there's a life out there that is available to us, and it's a good, abundant life, but we might or might not achieve it? Dang! Okay, so we have to figure out how to have this abundant life. Let's do it.

FICKLE FEELINGS

*"The world is full of suffering, but it
is also full of overcoming it."*
—HELEN KELLER

*"I don't want to be at the mercy of my emotions. I want
to use them, to enjoy them, and to dominate them."*
—OSCAR WILDE[2]

---

2 Oscar Wilde, *The Picture of Dorian Gray* (New York, NY: Randon House, 2004).

IF YOU DON'T *FIGHT,* THEN YOU DON'T *WIN*

*H*elen Keller was an author, activist, and educator whose lifetime of public advocacy for many communities and causes had lasting global impact. However, she was blind and deaf as a result of a childhood trauma. From a young age, she was handicapped and automatically launched into life with all of the odds stacked against her. Despite the probability of her never learning, she was the first deaf-blind person to receive a bachelor of arts degree and not from just *any* college—but a Harvard college. She was delayed in learning to communicate, but she was not deterred. She didn't let it stop her, eventually giving lectures and speeches and writing fourteen books. Her journey was a remarkable one, and here we are in 2023 *still* celebrating her life and accomplishments.

Michael Jordan is known as one of the greatest athletes of all time. Throughout his basketball career, he never lost three games in a row. He not only played in the National Basketball Association (NBA) but on Olympic teams as well before being inducted into the Naismith Memorial Basketball Hall of Fame

IF YOU DON'T *FIGHT,* THEN YOU DON'T *WIN*

in April 2009. He is the first player in the NBA to become the majority owner of an NBA team.[3] He has starred in movies, and his net worth now is over two billion dollars. Despite all of these amazing accolades, after doing some research and internet surfing, I learned that all of the comments are not so great.

Michael Jordan continues to hold the title as one of the greatest athletes of all time, even after his permanent retirement. However, despite his remarkable talent on the court, he is not considered to be as classy as other professional athletes of his caliber.[4] Perhaps it's due to Michael Jordan's excessive gambling habits, which, although they are well-known now, were constantly swept under the rug by his PR team and managers. He was also noted for having several extramarital affairs, which he paid off to keep hidden from the public during his career.[5] How had he dealt with his issues? I love this quote: "Obstacles don't have to stop you. If you run into a wall, don't turn around and give up. Figure out how to climb it, go through it, or work around it."[6]

What wall have you hit? Or should I say what mountain is standing in your way of being who you were created to be? Take the GOAT's (greatest of all time—it's my book, so it's my

---

[3] Staff, Editorial, et al., "60 Interesting Michael Jordan Facts You Should Know," *The Fact File*, 26 Mar. 2022, thefactfile.org/michael-jordan-facts/.
[4] Benny Vargas, "Don't Confuse Greatness with Class: Why Michael Jordan Is No DiMaggio." *Bleacher Report*, 3 Oct. 2017, bleacherreport.com/articles/423366-do-not-confuse-greatness-with-class-why-jordan-should-shut-his-mouth.
[5] Brian Quevedo, "His Affairs and Other Things Michael Jordan Wishes Would Disappear," *TheThings*, 27 Apr. 2020, www.thethings.com/his-affairs-and-other-things-michael-jordan-wishes-would-disappear/#the-cheap-owner-story.
[6] "Michael Jordan: 10 Quotes on His Birthday," *The Christian Science Monitor*, 19 Feb. 2013, www.csmonitor.com/USA/Sports/2013/0219/Michael-Jordan-10-quotes-from-His-Airness-the-King/On-obstacles.

opinion—I choose Michael) advice: climb it, go through it, or work around it, but DO NOT GIVE UP.

> What wall have you hit? Or should I say what mountain is standing in your way of being who you were created to be?

Jamie Kern Lima is a best-selling author and billionaire who landed on summer's *Forbes* "America's Richest Self-Made Women" list.[7] However, she has not always been on top of the world. She was told no over and over by multiple investors because of her looks and weight. Jamie is a gorgeous woman, but she had rosacea, and, in those years, the makeup industry only used flawless models. She wanted to create a makeup brand for the flawed women of the world—one that tried to help those of us who don't have perfect skin. The makeup industry fought her at every turn, but she did not take no for an answer. In her book *Believe IT,* she says, "When I started to see my fear staring back at me, I knew that I had to make my faith bigger than my fear."[8] Today, because of her grit, perseverance, and faith in her

---
7 Kerry A. Dolan and Luisa Kroll With Andrea Murphy, "America's Richest Self-Made Women 2023." *Forbes,* 1 June 2023, www.forbes.com/self-made-women/?sh=7d7326926d96.
8 Jamie Kern Lima, *Believe It: How to Go from Underestimated to Unstoppable* (New York, NY: Gallery Books, 2021).

IF YOU DON'T *FIGHT,* THEN YOU DON'T *WIN*

God, she's successful. After all, she sold her makeup company, IT Cosmetics, to L'Oréal for $1.2 billion dollars! Yes! Billion!

Keller, Jordan, Lima and thousands of other amazing people chose not to take no for an answer. Instead, they pursued their dreams in the face of adversity, setbacks, humiliation, addictions, handicaps, divorce, bankruptcy, bullying, bad skin, speech defects, weird tongues, warts, acne, and cellulite. And the list goes on! It would've been so easy for Helen Keller's parents to just concede that she would never do what other children could do. But they didn't. They had a choice and didn't take the path of least resistance. It had to be so difficult for her to be thrown into a school environment with "normal" children who automatically knew that THAT was an apple. She had never *seen* an apple or *heard* the word apple. Think about that for a minute.

It would've been easy for Michael Jordan to have never come back to the NBA when he faced the additional setback of losing his father. He could've been so overcome with grief that feeling happy again and making others happy seemed a million miles away. He could've never recovered from his divorce and never found love again, but he *did* recover, and he *did* pull himself out of the grief from those awful losses, and he went on to be one of the greatest of all times. Some would argue THE greatest of all time.

Jamie Kern Lima . . . Ahhh! Such an inspiration to women of all shapes and sizes with freckles, rosacea, and big pores. She was determined to break the "beauty mold" of flawless skin and a size-2 body, even when all of the beauty and cosmetic world said no, and she did it. It was an awful journey of being put down, laughed at, bullied, and not believed in. But she went from underestimated to unstoppable. SHE DID IT!

These are just three people we probably all know or have read about or heard of, but there are many other comeback stories that give me hope to get up and keep going when I really want to eat four bags of chips with dip, never shave my legs again, and morph into a greasy couch potato. My feelings cannot and should not dictate my actions or my lack of action. If I went by my feelings most days, I would've never finished writing this book. I might have ended up on a beach selling margaritas when my marriage fell apart. I probably would've never shown my face again in public. I would've gone into hiding. BUT I DIDN'T LET MY FEELINGS DICTATE MY ACTIONS.

> **Feelings are a funny thing. My feelings change so often about so many different things.... We can be really fickle and really undependable, can't we?**

Feelings are a funny thing. My feelings change so often about so many different things. Sometimes, I feel like it's okay to voice my opinion on social media, and other times, I feel like that's

IF YOU DON'T *FIGHT,* THEN YOU DON'T *WIN*

probably not a good idea. Sometimes, I feel like I want chili cheeseburgers and french fries four out of the seven days, and then, other days, I feel like I need to do a colon cleanse. Sometimes, I feel like everyone on earth is looney (except me), and the other days, I feel so much compassion for the needs and pain of hurting people. We can be really fickle and really undependable, can't we? All because of how we FEEL or don't feel on any given day.

The Bible has some really strong things to say about people who are up and down, in and out, hot and cold—fickle people:

> If any of you lacks wisdom, you should ask God, who gives generously to all without finding fault, and it will be given to you. But when you ask, you must believe and not doubt, because the one who doubts is like a wave of the sea, blown and tossed by the wind. That person should not expect to receive anything from the Lord. Such a person is double-minded and unstable in all they do."—James 1:5-8

Ouch! And there are more scriptures on this subject. Matthew 5:37 admonishes us, "All you need to say is simply 'Yes' or 'No'; anything beyond this comes from the evil one." Double ouch! So, when we're up and down, tossed about in our feelings, we aren't being led by the Spirit of God but the evil one, and according to James 1:17, we shouldn't expect to receive anything from the Lord—who only gives good things. We've got to unpack this. Let's do it.

HOPE CARPENTER

The truth is, none of us set out into adulthood WANTING to be la-la-losers. Every single one of us WANTS to be great. We all want to be successful, happy, fulfilled, and purposeful. The HOW is the problem. We've been launched into adulthood with so many holes and issues from the way we were raised. Maybe our handicaps attracted the bullies of the world. Then, being bullied put fear in our hearts and drained our self-esteem. What about not making the proper scores on the SAT? That hindered us from going to college to get the proper degrees to be hired for a higher-paying job.

Or what if the whole issue with *that* is that we didn't have a parent at home because they had to work two or three jobs to make ends meet and had no oversight to make sure that we studied to make good grades SO THAT we could have the ability to do well on those crazy standardized tests? Many variables go into how we are launched out into adulthood, where push comes to shove, and only the strong survive.

From here, our negative self-talk and beliefs about ourselves cause us to have a victim mentality, and we spiral even further. So many things to overcome. We have to talk about these things because they literally hold us hostage, frozen with fear, doubt, shame, grief, and other feelings, second-guessing ourselves into a state of nothingness. And nothingness doesn't stay like that; we continue to drift and spiral downward because the truth is, we're either growing or dying. We don't just stay the same.

I've got big boy and big girl news for you: you couldn't help that those things happened to you, but you *are* responsible for what you do with them. Yes, life is hard. Yes, the way we were treated, the names we were called, the homes we grew up in, the lack of education and resources—all have affected us and made us who we are today. However, it is *our choice* whether we let it make us bitter or better. That's the bottom line. Now, let's get back to the concept of being double-minded we talked about earlier in this chapter. This will wrap it up for you.

Double-minded comes from the Greek word *dipsychos*, meaning a person has two minds or souls. James was saying that when we are double-minded, we are tossed about and unstable in all we do. Our minds are very powerful because they are where we really serve the Lord. Scripture tells us that our minds must be set on things above where Christ is (see Colossians 3:2). What that means is that we must take our minds, our thoughts, and meditate (think) the way God does. We must think and say what God says about any given situation—not what *we* think or feel.

> We must take our minds, our thoughts, and meditate (think) the way God does. We must think and say what God says about any given situation—not what we think or feel.

HOPE CARPENTER

Double-mindedness happens when we are people of faith one day and people of doubt the next. We are motivated one day and lazy the next. We are disciplined one day and eat the #5 supersized combo the next day and maybe the next day. We are faithful in our giving and tithing one month and greedy and fearful that God won't provide for us the next month. Are you getting the concept?

Do you remember me telling you about Ron's workout regimen? How he works out no matter where he is on the planet, whether the gym has the right equipment, and regardless of whether he's jet-lagged or tired? He decided a long time ago that working out would be a part of his daily life because it was that important to his well-being, health, and stress relief. He made that decision one time, and he has been diligent, faithful, and consistent. Because of that, the benefits are clear: he's physically fit, disciplined, and has better health results than people who do not exercise regularly. Because he doesn't waver (or is double-minded), he gets results.

Honestly, this is a very deep concept, and I could go down a rabbit hole right here and I won't, but I will elaborate on the concept of integrity. Integrity comes from the word "integrated" which means all the parts are linked or coordinated. Another definition is, to bring together or incorporate (parts) into a whole. To make up, combine, or complete to produce a whole or larger unit, as parts do. O.M.G. Just mull over that for a minute when thinking about the concept of doublemindedness. Being a person of "integrity" is being a person where all

IF YOU DON'T *FIGHT,* THEN YOU DON'T *WIN*

the "parts" combine—a person who does what they say, says what they really mean, a person who is dependable because everything matches.

My question to you is this: Are you a person of integrity? *Really,* a person of integrity. We might think we are because we don't cheat, get drunk, or hit our spouse (you know, all the big sins), but integrity is where EVERY PART matches. We can't *say* we love God but hate our brothers and sisters. We can't *say* we want a good marriage but never do the necessary things that produce a good, healthy marriage. We can't *say* we trust God with our lives but withhold our giving and live in fear anytime a pandemic breaks out. That, my precious friend, is double-minded.

God wants you to live a beautiful, abundant life. He has already done everything on His end for you to achieve it, but that's just it. His part is over. Now, it's your turn to keep your end of the bargain. Are you pursuing wholeness and freedom from your childhood pain, your poor choices, your negativity—your double-mindedness? Or are you agreeing with your past and nurturing your pain? God is not a genie in a bottle or a magician who is going to wave a magic wand over your life and make everything easy. An amazing life is available for every one of us, but there is much work to be done to achieve it. Do you have what it takes? Only your choices will answer that.

WE HAVE AN ENEMY—BE AWARE

"When you are thoroughly conversant with strategy, you will recognize the enemy's intentions and thus have many opportunities to win."
—MIYAMOTO MUSASHI[9]

"We often give our enemies the means of our own destruction."
—AESOP

---

9 Miyamoto Musashi, *Book of Five Rings* (Toledo, OH: Cedar Lake Publishing, 2022).

IF YOU DON'T *FIGHT,* THEN YOU DON'T *WIN*

We ended chapter 2 on the topic of working out, so let's pick up with that topic as an example. I heard a podcast not long ago from Simon Sinek. He was talking about commitment, and the gist of his talk was this: If you go to the gym today and go home and look in the mirror, you will see nothing. If you go to the gym the next few days and work out and go home and look in the mirror, you will see no change. You'll think, *This doesn't work,* and you'll quit. But if you keep going to the gym, eventually, you will see results. If you stick with it consistently, you will get in shape and see its effects.

You might slip up and eat tons of chocolate one night or get sick and skip a day or two, but if you don't throw your hands up and quit, you *will* see results. It's all about perseverance and consistency! Remember I said that I want to be like Ron when I grow up? Well, I'm not a gym rat like him, and I have pretty much resigned myself to the fact that I'll never have a chiseled body. Why? Because I do not want one. That sounds so strange, right? Why wouldn't I want a toned, chiseled body? Do

IF YOU DON'T *FIGHT,* THEN YOU DON'T *WIN*

I want to be chunky and fluffy? Obviously, I do. Why? Because I CHOOSE not to go to the gym or do what it takes to have that kind of physique.

> **Our lives are the sum of the choices we make.**

Our lives are the sum of the choices we make. I can say all day long that I hate my cellulite, and I want to have nice toned legs, but until I *want* the toned legs more than I *want* to eat chips and dip, french fries, and tiramisu, then I'm just double-minded. If I wanted it bad enough, I'd go for it. And that translates to every choice I'm faced with in life. Is the prize worth the process? I can say I want a good marriage, but until I'm willing to learn what a good marriage looks like and be willing to shift, grow, submit, shut my mouth, serve my mate, forgive over and over, crucify my flesh, and all the other *hard things* that go into a great relationship, I'll just have an average, at best, marriage—that I most likely hate.

I think that we have bought into the lie that being a Christian means that you're never supposed to have problems. That once we make the decision to accept Jesus into our lives and embrace Christianity, tulips are supposed to pop up everywhere we walk, and it never rains on our parade again. That's just not true.

HOPE CARPENTER

Quite the contrary. Once you start walking with the Lord, on the Lord's side, you have engaged your enemy who hates you and does not want you to live a victorious life. So, what does he do? He comes to steal from you, killing your hopes and dreams, and tries to destroy everything in your life. He is relentless in his pursuit of you. He does not care what kind of day you've had or how much sleep you got last night. He's still coming for you.

You have to understand that you are called according to a purpose. God has a purpose and a plan for the life of every human being walking the earth, but you have an enemy with an assignment to disrupt your assignment. It's like the back and forth of a football game. One team has the ball, and they are trying to make advances into the end zone so that they score, but there is another team, with just as much determination to stop the offense from gaining ground.

In this situation, you have to ask yourself several questions. The first one is this: Do you have a plan? Have you practiced and studied your opponent to know how he moves and what his tactics are? Then, do you know you: your flaws, weaknesses, strengths, tendencies, etc.? Finally, have you counted the cost? There is a story in the Bible that says, hold on, let me allow you to read it for yourself:

> Large crowds were traveling with Jesus, and turning to them he said: "If anyone comes to me and does not hate father and mother, wife and children, brothers and sisters—yes, even their own life—such a person cannot

IF YOU DON'T *FIGHT,* THEN YOU DON'T *WIN*

> be my disciple. And whoever does not carry their cross and follow me cannot be my disciple.
>
> "Suppose one of you wants to build a tower. Won't you first sit down and estimate the cost to see if you have enough money to complete it? For if you lay the foundation and are not able to finish it, everyone who sees it will ridicule you, saying, 'This person began to build and wasn't able to finish.'
>
> "Or suppose a king is about to go to war against another king. Won't he first sit down and consider whether he is able with ten thousand men to oppose the one coming against him with twenty thousand? If he is not able, he will send a delegation while the other is still a long way off and will ask for terms of peace. In the same way, those of you who do not give up everything you have cannot be my disciples." —Luke 14:25-33

In this text, Jesus is encouraging his followers to really think about and examine what it means to follow Him because clearly, they did not understand what would be required. Jesus is trying to show them that they need to forsake everything in their lives in order to follow Him, and He did it by using the examples in the text: building a tower and going to war. The point He was trying to get across is this: if you want to succeed, start at the beginning. You don't just *happen* to succeed; you plan to succeed. And one part of planning to succeed is knowing whom you're fighting.

You have an enemy, the devil. He hates you. He wants to see you fail. He will not take it easy on you. He will use your failures, your past, your deficiencies, your weaknesses—whatever—and he doesn't care what you think or how you feel about it. That is his job, and he is the best at what he does. You have to be on the offensive in the game of life at all times. You must wake up every day and put on the armor of God because, ladies and gentlemen, we are at war. War for what? Our purpose to be walked out here on earth.

> **You don't just happen to succeed; you plan to succeed.**

War is terrifying, bloody, and exhausting. Believe it or not, I like war movies; they have always fascinated me. The culmination of all war movies is the actual war, but there is much preparation and training that must take place long before the first bullet is fired. It requires submission to authority (even if you don't like them or agree with them), willingness to do whatever is asked of you by your superiors, and discipline it takes to be strong physically, mentally, and emotionally to get through rigorous exercise and days with no sleep or food. Not to mention the physical pain and exertion it takes to endure extreme climates, climbing, running, etc., and so much more that I have no clue about. War is brutal, and we are in a war with the enemy. The battle is over our destiny.

Hope, this is so hard! This is entirely too much work! Yeah, I wish it were easy, but it's not, and the quicker we embrace

IF YOU DON'T *FIGHT,* THEN YOU DON'T *WIN*

this—the truth that *life is hard*—the quicker we can start advancing toward our best life. The life that is available to every one of us.

I did not take all of this time discussing our enemy so that we can become fearful of him or to make him out to be more powerful than we are. I took the time to make sure that you know that you have one, and he is working constantly to try to trip you up so that you will get so discouraged that you won't even try.

Ron was preaching one Sunday, and he used this example to explain how the enemy works in our lives. It's called "broken focus." Have you ever been to the circus and seen the massive lions, who could take us out with one snap of the jaw, standing on the circular table under the instruction of the little guy with the tiny whip in his hand? Think about it: the king of the jungle, known for his strength, power, and ferocity and weighing up to five hundred pounds, standing there, not moving, because of a tiny little ringmaster. Why is the lion not ripping this guy to shreds? I'm glad you asked.

The lion is so focused on balancing that he is not even concerned with the ringmaster or, more importantly, His lion-ability. You see, the ringmaster is clever. He has that huge beast on a table with only three legs, and if the lion shifts or moves the wrong way, he will become unbalanced and fall. The lion is so focused on balancing that he can't even be good at what he's created to do—hunt, destroy, and eat. Our enemy is just like this ringmaster. He is clever and cunning; he knows what we're good at and where we are weak, and he targets the areas of our weakness. He knows all about you, so you'd better become wise to his schemes. Wake up every day on the offense. If you really want to win in life, you have to count the cost and know whom and why you're fighting. You have an enemy, and he wants to steal, kill, and destroy you (John 10:10) so that you will never walk out your purpose.

You may be thinking about your life right now, and you feel so discouraged about where you are. That *should* be your response if you are not walking in your God-given calling and purpose. I remember, after Ron and I married, we rented an old house in the bad part of town because, at the time, it was all we could afford. It was over one hundred years old, and it smelled like it, looked like it, and we had a lot of work to do to even make it livable. We were only renting but we still wanted to do what we could to make it better. We painted, put new carpet in, and spent many hours on the yard trimming trees that were originally bushes and pulling weeds and briars because "our standard" was better than the standard of the house's present condition. I remember Ron would look at that house and say out loud, "You can't hold me, and I won't live here all my life." Did he think that he was better than the other people who lived in that neighborhood? Not necessarily, but he did know that being a son of the most, high God provided him privileges and he was determined to have every privilege that God's Word said that we could have. We were only in our twenties during that time, but we had enough God-sense that we never despised the day of small beginnings (see Zechariah 4:10). We embraced our season and circumstance and

IF YOU DON'T *FIGHT,* THEN YOU DON'T *WIN*

CHOSE to make the best of it. If it was broken, we fixed it. If it was stinky, we sprayed Lysol. If it needed paint, we painted it. We might not have had much but what we had was pristine. Why? Because we had God-potential on the inside of us that drove us to live on a God-kind of level. I believe as a child of God, there is God-potential on the inside of us that is screaming to get out. We are His children. His lifeblood flows through our veins, and that is why normal, common, less than, or average will never satisfy. God has something unique and special for every one of us to do, but even though we might be naturally inclined to do it, we don't because of all the baggage we carry around. We've believed lies from the enemy or even from people that we don't deserve more or that "more" isn't necessary, but that's just a lie from the pit of hell. He never promised that this type of life would be easy. In our walk with the Lord, He will always require us to operate in faith. Faith, by its very nature, causes you to operate on a level that you presently do not have. Living by faith means that you don't see, hear, smell, taste, or touch the thing that you're desiring or reaching for and until you live like **that,** you're not pleasing God.

Hebrews 11:16 states, "And without faith it is impossible to please God, because anyone who comes to Him must believe that He exists and that He rewards those who earnestly seek Him." Here's the thing about faith; it will always require you to launch out, to start, without all of the information. It takes faith to start a business without large amounts of money in the bank. It takes faith to quit your job, pack up your belongings, and move to another country as a missionary. It takes faith to start a church in a warehouse with only three people, an old upright piano that won't stay tuned, and no hope of anyone ever showing up.

> **We are God's children. His lifeblood flows through our veins, and that is why normal, common, less than, or average will never satisfy.**

I heard a wonderful saying not long ago about life being hard, but it's also hard to change whatever "hard" circumstance you're in. The saying is called "Choose Your Hard."

> Marriage is hard. Divorce is hard. *Choose your hard.*
>
> Obesity is hard. Being fit is hard. *Choose your hard.*
>
> Being in debt is hard. Being financially disciplined is hard. *Choose your hard.*
>
> Communication is hard. Not communicating is hard. *Choose your hard.*
>
> Life will never be easy. It will always be hard. But we can choose our hard.
>
> *Pick wisely.* —Unknown

IF YOU DON'T *FIGHT,* THEN YOU DON'T *WIN*

This is just so good. It's so accurate. I had to choose my hard about ten years ago in the arena of my marriage. It was 2013 when my life came crumbling down all around me on a very public stage, and it seemed like there was no way to fix it. Too much had happened. I had hurt too many people throughout too many years of dishonesty. Trust was shattered. It seemed so much easier to just concede that it was over and move on, but I loved my husband, and I wanted so desperately to do whatever it would take to try to fix my marriage. Being alone and single with no church family, no job, a bad reputation, no money, and worst of all, no family was going to be so difficult. Trying to pick up the broken pieces, walking in humility, owning my issues, trying to rebuild trust, being scrutinized, paying restitution, and the list goes on and on, were going to be so difficult. I was warned that it could take years and years (and it did).

Both were going to be hard, but I had to choose the hard that was God-ordained for my life. What was God's path for me? What hard was a part of my purpose that God wanted to use for my good and His glory? He never promised us that our road would be without pain, but He did promise to never leave us nor forsake us on this hard journey. I've found the old saying, "What doesn't kill you makes you stronger" to be accurate. There have been things in my life that were SO HARD and so painful and seemed so impossible that I thought I'd never make it out alive, but—NEWS FLASH—here I am. That is how I can so passionately write the words on these pages to try to show you that if you'll just muster up enough strength to keep swinging, you'll make it out alive too. And not just make it out alive but come out on the other side bigger, better, stronger, and wiser.

I love the Bible for many reasons, but one is that we can look to our forefathers and their lives as examples for us today. When we are afraid or uncertain, we can find hope in God's Word to help us push forward and keep fighting our own good fight. There is probably no one in the Bible who suffered more than Job. He had everything that we would consider "good": a family, a good name, tons of wealth, etc. Satan asked permission to go after Job to test him. He struck Job's family, livelihood (crops and livestock), health, and all of his relationships that were left.

Let's just all be honest right now and think about how we would've responded if that had happened to us. We think we have it bad when the dishwasher goes out, and we have to wash the dishes by hand. Or what about our internet going out, and we can't watch our favorite shows or, God forbid, our favorite football team play? What if you were stricken with a deadly disease, every one of your children was murdered, and all of your wealth and resources to gain wealth were stolen from you? How would you respond? What would be your thoughts toward God?

Well, Job didn't curse God, and he didn't lose his faith in God. He responded with worship:

> At this, Job got up and tore his robe and shaved his head. Then he fell to the ground in worship and said: "Naked I come from my mother's womb, and naked I will depart. The Lord gave and the Lord has taken away; may the name of the Lord be praised."—Job 1:20-21

IF YOU DON'T *FIGHT,* THEN YOU DON'T *WIN*

Job questioned God and asked why, but he humbled himself and never cursed or blamed Him, and God gave him back twice as much as he had lost. God, being our heavenly Father, is such a great Father, and He is always using our situations and circumstances to shape, mold, and teach us if we will embrace Him as our good Father and Master Teacher.

> God, being our heavenly Father, is such a great Father, and He is always using our situations and circumstances to shape, mold, and teach us if we will embrace Him as our good Father and Master Teacher.

Look at King David's life; he was no stranger to difficult times, either. He was chosen by God and anointed by the prophet Samuel to be Israel's king, but for many years of his life, he was also tormented, chased down, and on the run from King Saul. He had to live in caves and gather men to help, aid, and support him. What was David's response during this time? He could've killed Saul many times, but he didn't; he kept his heart pure before God, and God rewarded him. Saul eventually fell on his own sword. Did David get tired, frustrated, and desperate? Yes! He cried out in Psalm 142:1-2, "I cry aloud to the Lord; I lift up my voice to the Lord for mercy. I pour out before him my complaint; before him I tell my trouble." David, just like Job, got tired, but he never lost his faith. He brought his wandering thoughts back to their core, their center, and that was his faith in God.

I have found that God delights in using broken things. If it makes sense, it's usually not God. He never does what's easy because He gets no glory that way. Why did God use a virgin to birth Jesus? That made no sense. Jesus stands in front of a tomb and commands the dead to come forth; that makes no sense. If it's easy and makes sense, it's usually not God. Whenever it's hard and makes no sense, it's God. When you're broke and God asks for your last dollar, it's God. When you're forty years old and finally getting married and you know God told you you're going to have children, it's God. When God tells you to pack up and move to another city, away from everything familiar, but you know your blessing is in that city, it's God. Faith will always be required in this journey to become who you were created to be; nothing will ever be easy. You might as well resign to the fact that you will be water-walking the entire journey. Don't let the struggle derail you, rather, let it fuel you.

You have an enemy who wants to keep you so focused on the problems in your life—just like that ringmaster and the lion—that you take your eyes off the one who holds your future in His hands. There's a lion inside of you! God's DNA is flowing through your veins. Problems will come. Trouble is a part of

IF YOU DON'T *FIGHT,* THEN YOU DON'T *WIN*

all of our journeys, but don't take your eyes off of Jesus, and don't allow the trouble to make you lose heart. You will reap the reward IF you don't lose heart. Your enemy stirs up a lot of trouble, but he is also a liar, and he knows that in the end, he loses, and we win.

PRESSURE PRODUCES IF YOU LET IT

"God changes caterpillars into butterflies, sand into pearls and coal into diamonds using time and pressure. He's working on you, too."
—RICK WARREN[10]

"Everything negative—pressure, challenges— is all an opportunity for me to rise."
—KOBE BRYANT[11]

---

10 Rick Warren, Twitter post, April 15, 2011, 5:32 pm, https://twitter.com/RickWarren/status/59006112120315904?lang=en.
11 Kobi Highlights and Motivation, Twitter post, August 31, 2022, 10:49 am, https://twitter.com/kobehighlight/status/1564988802606673923?lang=en.

IF YOU DON'T *FIGHT*, THEN YOU DON'T *WIN*

The feeling of pressure or being under pressure is not a good feeling. Our bodies change physically under pressure as our sympathetic nervous system begins sending signals to the adrenal glands causing them to produce adrenaline and cortisol that cause us to breathe heavily and sweat excessively. Our anxiety goes through the roof, and we spend many sleepless nights as our mind races. Pressure seems to produce anything but good.

I remember one of my college courses was public speaking, and we had to get up before the class and give speeches that we'd prepared. There was no rhyme or reason to the order we gave them. We were called on randomly, as the teacher saw fit. Just walking into the classroom, I would begin to feel anxiety. *What if it's my turn today to be called upon to stand in front of all these scared people and talk?* I didn't want to make eye contact with the professor but thought, *If I act involved and be the super-attentive student, maybe he will pick on someone else, and I'll get through another day unscathed.*

IF YOU DON'T *FIGHT,* THEN YOU DON'T *WIN*

We've talked about the physical changes that happen when we are under pressure, but what about the brain? The nervous system is constantly relaying information to the brain and to the body, almost like a loop. So, whatever your physical body is feeling, the brain, thinking about it all seems to magnify the feelings. This is what causes athletes to fall, drop balls, and miss free throws—athletes who would *never* fall, drop balls, or miss shots.

The vagus nerve has the job of informing the brain exactly how activated our body is for the sole purpose of managing stress and pressure. Why is this important? Because in extreme situations, our body's messages can overwhelm thought-based interventions.[12] Here's a very practical example: You're lying in bed, and you wake up to a loud noise. Your heart starts racing, and immediately you're thinking, *Where is the gun? Someone is in my house!* You try to calm yourself down by saying, "No one is in the house; it was probably just the cat," but your vagus nerve is telling your brain that your heart is beating too fast, and your breathing needs to be controlled. What does your brain listen to? Yes! Your overbeating heart, saying something's not right, and it's probably Jason from Friday the 13th coming down the hall with his machete.

I said all that to say this: stress and pressure, if not harnessed, can harm us, paralyze us, and ultimately destroy us. That kind of stress and pressure keeps us stagnant and unproductive,

---

[12] Dane Jensen, *The Power of Pressure Why We Break down and What We Can Learn from Those Who Break Through* (Ontario Canada: HarperCollins, 2021) 35.

even when we know we're not the only ones afraid of giving the speech and that Jason is not even real. This is how we get locked out of the good life. We let the fear of "What if?" keep us from even trying.

> **Stress and pressure, if not harnessed, can harm us, paralyze us, and ultimately destroy us.**

There is a kind of pressure that works for us if we will allow it to. Everyone reading this went to a science class in elementary school and learned about how a caterpillar turns into a butterfly, right? It's so interesting to me. The butterfly lays her eggs on a leaf or branch. When it's time, the caterpillar breaks out of its egg, eats the shell that it emerged from, and then eats the leaf it was hatched on. Mr. Caterpillar is so hungry it just eats and eats and grows and grows out of his exoskeleton several times over. (He's too big for his own britches. Sorry, I just had to.) He then finds a branch, hangs upside down, and moves out of his exoskeleton until it forms a chrysalis where he isn't a caterpillar or a butterfly anymore but a pupa. In the pupa stage, for about ten days, it grows six legs and adds an antennae and wings. Then the butterfly hatches his way out to be the beautiful creature we

IF YOU DON'T *FIGHT,* THEN YOU DON'T *WIN*

all know and love. That beauty did not come without pressure, time, and growth.

Our life will be full of times of stretching, growing, learning, crawling to walking and then running, but if we aren't willing to GO THROUGH the process, which can be painful at times, we will never bloom into the beautiful creature God has ordained us to be. I love this quote by Joseph B. Wirthlin, "As with the butterfly, adversity is necessary to build character in people."[13] I can look back over some of the most painful times in my life, and it's true. Adversity and struggle will make you into something powerful if you let the struggle work something *in you*.

"Diamonds are a girl's best friend," some would say. What makes them so rare and pricey? Are they easy to find? Are they easy to make? Heck no. Just the opposite.

- » Bury carbon dioxide 100 miles into Earth.
- » Heat it to about 2,200 degrees Fahrenheit.
- » Squeeze it under a pressure of 725,000 pounds per square inch.
- » Then quickly rush to Earth's surface to cool.

I'd say that's a process. Wouldn't you? Hundreds of miles underground where tremendous amounts of heat and pressure are used to crystalize carbon into rough diamonds. The miners don't just go out there with a shovel and bucket and say, "Looky here! There's a diamond." No! There are volcanic eruptions or blasts with heavy machinery, and all of this is very risky,

---

[13] Elder Joseph B. Wirthlin, "Finding a Safe Harbor," *The Church of Jesus Christ of Latter-Day Saints*, 2 Apr. 2000, www.churchofjesuschrist.org/study/gsneral-conference/2000/04/finding-a-safe-harbor?lang=eng.

especially when underground mining is required. After this, there has to be crushing and milling to break the ore. There are so many steps in the mining and refining process that are way over my college experience, so I'm hoping you get the picture. Without that process, there wouldn't be glistening, shiny diamonds that thousands and thousands of people all over the world are paying top dollar for. Diamonds are valuable because they are precious. There has been a high price paid to have this beautiful rock draped around our necks, perched on our fingers, and for some, glittering on our teeth. We love them, but if they weren't so costly, we wouldn't want them or desire them.

Diamonds are formed after high temperature and extreme pressure are applied, and even then, it takes a matter of time—up to millions of years—to materialize. Becoming great is not an overnight process nor is it easy or glamorous. Pain is inevitable. Jesus never promised easy, but He did promise to be with us and to never leave us nor forsake us.

Again, we all know that I'm no fitness lover, but I also know a bit of biology and what it takes to make a muscle strong. When YOU, not I, go to the gym to exercise, as you lift weights, especially strength training, it forces the muscles' fibers to contract and stretch over and over. This causes tiny tears in the fabric of the muscle; the size of these tears depends on the intensity of the exercise. When you stop the exercise and go back home, the muscle is now in the recovery process where satellite cells repair those tears. They replicate, mature, and fuse to the damaged muscle fibers, forming a new muscle protein strand that

IF YOU DON'T *FIGHT,* THEN YOU DON'T *WIN*

increases the size and strength of the muscle to ensure it can keep up with future demand. Exercise, therefore, exposes your muscles to a form of stress known as eustress, which may be painful in the short term but will lead to greater long-term gains. (Lord, I'm about to run all over this house!) The rest period is when the body rebuilds muscle so that it is bigger and stronger than before.[14] Did you hear that? Bigger. Stronger. Better than before!

I don't know if you've ever birthed a child, but I have birthed three. Most studies show that the number of humans ever born is probably around eighty billion. Yes, billion. Now, we all know that creating, gestating, and birthing another whole human is just a sheer miracle in itself, but the pain of the birthing process is what I want to focus on for a few minutes. It wasn't until the 1800s that medicine was used to aid in the pain of childbirth. Chloroform, morphine, anesthesia, hallucinogens, epidurals, and such have been used to try to ease the severe pain of pushing another human out of the body. Clearly, there is tremendous pain in bringing children into the world, or these types of drugs would have never been used. Women scream, vomit, pass out, break hips, and lose enormous amounts of blood. Would you like to hear more, or do you get the picture?

Even with this type of pain, women still birth babies. Here's the thing: women go to massive lengths to be able to have children. They lose weight and get on vitamins. Some pay large amounts of money for invitro-fertilization. They go through

---

14 "What Happens to Your Muscles during Exercise and Recovery?" *Breathing Labs*, 30 Apr. 1970, www.breathinglabs.com/sports-athletics/what-happens-to-your-muscles-during-exercise-and-recovery/.

the process of retrieving eggs and storing them (not taking into account the monetary expense of all of this). They do all of this and so much more just to have children. Do they go into the planning and process of getting pregnant with the horrendous physical pain in mind? No. Why? The prize is worth the process. All mothers know that pain is a part of the process, but the pain never keeps us from getting what we want, the baby. Even after having babies, I would say 100 percent that it was nothing in comparison to the joy of what that pain produced. There will be painful things in life that we must go through to be able to hold precious things in our hands. No rain, no flowers. No thorns, no roses. No pain, no gain.

> There will be painful things in life that we must go through to be able to hold precious things in our hands. No rain, no flowers. No thorns, no roses. No pain, no gain.

Life is going to throw you some curve balls, fast pitches, foul balls, and might even pop you upside the head. We face things that we never dreamed that we would have to face when we were that little girl playing Ken and Barbie, dreaming of living in

IF YOU DON'T *FIGHT,* THEN YOU DON'T *WIN*

a castle and galloping off into the sunset together with our tall, dark, handsome, and brave knight. Life can feel unfair at times when the trouble we face feels like a stab in the back and cruel and unusual punishment. But here's what we must remember during these dark, confusing, and painful times in our lives: we only have one choice, and that is to know-that-we-know that we serve a *good* God who is for us and not against us. We can believe scripture:

> No temptation has overtaken you except what is common to mankind. And God is faithful; he will not let you be tempted beyond what you can bear. But when you are tempted, he will also provide a way out so that you can endure it.—1 Corinthians 10:13

I don't know why we doubt the goodness and faithfulness of God when trouble hits our lives. If we would just sit and think back over our lives, as far as we can remember, of all of the situations and circumstances that we THOUGHT at the time would literally take us out, and they didn't! We made it through. God has proven faithful time and time again, yet we continue to freak out, half lose our minds, go into panic mode, and seem to get amnesia about all the times and ways God has been so faithful to us. What is wrong with us? Have you ever stopped to think about all the difficult times? Even though we hated it at the time, looking back, we can 100 percent say that those times worked FOR us and not AGAINST us. Pressure *does produce!*

HOPE CARPENTER

We only have one life, and the Bible compares it to a race. The goal in the race is to win or finish well. The end goal of salvation is eternal life, but what about here on earth? Do we just be miserable and wait for the eternal payout? Heck no. When Jesus was teaching His disciples how to pray, he told them to pray this way: "Thy kingdom come. Thy will be done, ON EARTH as it is in HEAVEN" (Matthew 6:10, NASB, emphasis added). Our eternal security is not the only benefit of salvation; kingdom living is possible here on earth, but it will make demands on the runner.

We will not finish well if we are not whole, healthy, and free from bitterness at old hurts, strife, abuse, unforgiveness, hate, judgmentalism, and all the other yucky stuff. All of that will cause us to stumble on the track of life while we are trying to run our race. If our hearts are not healthy and strong enough, life will derail us. We will fall apart. We will trip and stumble—some of us more tragically than others. Some privately and some publicly, but we will all have those coming-off-the-track moments if we don't take the time to process pain.

Doctors will even tell you not to exert yourself too much if you have a physical heart condition. Why? You could collapse, have a heart attack, or even die. It's so important to take the necessary time to dig into the closets and corners of our hearts to clean out all of the painful moments that slow us down and hold us back from running at top speed. Just like we visit the doctor once a year for a physical check-up, to make sure everything is working right and our bloodwork is clean, we need to

IF YOU DON'T *FIGHT*, THEN YOU DON'T *WIN*

check in with a counselor, pastor, or mentor who can run the necessary tests and ask questions to ensure our emotional man is healthy. Do we ever reach a place called "There" where we are 100 percent spotless? Lord, no, but intentional maintenance does make a difference.

Philippians 1:6 (AMP) tells us, "I am convinced *and* confident of this very thing, that He who has begun a good work in you will [continue to] perfect *and* complete it until the day of Christ Jesus [the time of His return]." Read that again. Come on; just read it again. That ought to get you so excited and relieve you of some of the pressure that you've put on yourself to "glow in the dark for Jesus." Yes, we have a huge part to play in our relationship with Christ. We are the runners, but He also is in partnership with us while we run. This scripture tells us that there is a work going on inside of us developing, training, pruning, purging, building up, tearing down, deleting, retraining, etc., and the Bible says that this work is GOOD.

> Scripture tells us that there is a work going on inside of us developing, training, pruning, purging, building up, tearing down, deleting, retraining, etc., and the Bible says that this work is GOOD.

HOPE CARPENTER

The word work is translated in the Greek as "to toil" as an effort or occupation. That tells me that God's got a full-time job with us! But it comes with a retirement package—He gets us! He has put in so much effort, paid the penalty for our sins, all because He loves us and wants us to be with Him forever. He reaps the benefits of our winning; He reaps us! That's so humbling to me, that He loves us that much. Here's the thing: this "work" is a life-long process. A finished Christian is the result of years of training. Our salvation produces a babe in Christ, and then there is much spiritual nourishment, education, training, learning, growing, testing, failing, getting back up, etc., to develop the full-grown man and woman in Christ.

I don't know about you, but I was a hot mess when I gave my life to Christ, and I wished that someone would've told me this way back then, that I would have a life-long journey of "clean-up" in cooperation with the Holy Spirit. That would've saved me a lot of heartache to know that I was a new, spotless person, but, yes, my mind and emotions would still remember all that sin and heartache, and it would be a journey, for the rest of my life, to renew my mind so that I could walk out this great life God has for me. I'm not that good or that holy to think that I'm becoming more like Jesus on my own. It's a divine partnership with the Holy Spirit—*daily*—to be able to live this John 10:10 abundant life.

We must understand the nature and character of God and the implications of that character: God is not fickle that He should change, nor weak that He should fail, nor unfaithful that He

IF YOU DON'T *FIGHT,* THEN YOU DON'T *WIN*

would lie. He is working in us and promises to use everything on the outside to make sure the inside lines up with His purpose and plan for our lives. Think about it this way. Have you ever driven by a construction site where a large building is being erected, and alongside the building is scaffolding? You know, the metal platforms that are attached to the building itself? Scaffolding is not a part of the building, but it is used to build the building. That's exactly what God does with the pain and trouble in our lives; He uses it to build us, shape us, and mold us.

I heard a man on Instagram the other day talking about an article that he read about how lobsters grow. A lobster is a soft mushy animal that lives inside a rigid shell that doesn't move nor expand, so how does the lobster grow? As the lobster grows inside and expands, the shell becomes very confining and the lobster starts to feel very uncomfortable and restricted; he feels pressure, so he goes under the rocks to protect himself and cast off the shell to produce a new one. Well, eventually THAT shell is too small for the growing lobster, so he goes and does the same thing again and again and again. Here's the point: the stimulus for the lobster to grow is the pressure that makes him uncomfortable! He said something so interesting.

> If lobsters had doctors, they would never be able to grow because as soon as the lobster felt uncomfortable, he would go to the doctor to get a valium or a Xanax. He would feel better temporarily but never cast off the shell to grow. Times of stress and pressure are also times for growth.

HOPE CARPENTER

Whoa! This is called growing through what you go through.

So many times, in my life, trouble and pressure has been my master-teacher. I've learned so much about the nature of people, my own self, the nature of God, and the faithfulness of God, and it all came from difficult times. God is not just God. He is our heavenly Father. In general, a good father will sometimes have to make his child learn lessons and allow them to feel pain, spank their rear end, or put them in time-out—all because he knows more than the kid knows. He is doing a good work in that child. The child hates it and doesn't understand why the father would treat him that way. *Why would a good daddy take my privileges away or inflict pain on me?* BECAUSE HE LOVES YOU AND WANTS THE BEST FOR YOU. The Father knows it's working good in you.

Cooperation is key for this "good work" to be complete. We are partners in this education. This is so important. We've GOT to get this before we can go any further. We must exercise our faith and obedience in the strength of God and for the reception of God's work in us. This is what the title of this book means: IF YOU DON'T FIGHT, THEN YOU DON'T WIN. We've already talked about the enemy's tactics: divorce, rape, abandonment, abuse, burnout, addiction, mid-life crisis, and a million other things, all to get you to quit, right? Listen—those are the devil's tactics, but God uses all of those as His standard operating procedures. God uses all of them to strengthen us, grow us, and promote us.

IF YOU DON'T *FIGHT,* THEN YOU DON'T *WIN*

> **We must exercise our faith and obedience in the strength of God and for the reception of God's work in us.**

You can't have a victory without a battle. You can't graduate without a test, and here's the tricky thing about going through test time; the teacher doesn't talk during the test. A test, by its very nature, is designed to see what you ALREADY KNOW. When trouble/test time hits your life, do what you already know to do. If trouble hits your finances, keep giving. If trouble hits your relationships, live at peace as far as you can control, forgive quickly, and turn the other cheek. If trouble hits your health, plead the blood of Jesus, walk in faith, and speak the Word. Test time will also determine the length of the season you're in. If you don't pass the test, then you have to repeat the class. This is how we get stuck in cycles; we never learn the lessons, thus, we don't pass the test and there is no advancement in our lives.

We are commissioned to "fight the *good* fight of faith" (1 Timothy 6:12, NASB, emphasis added), and that word "good" is the same word that's used in the "good work" scripture above. This life will demand that you live by faith, but it's all good! Shout, "IT'S GOOD." Oops, sorry, I didn't know you were reading this on the subway or on the airplane or in the breakroom, lol.

HOPE CARPENTER

The most beautiful thing happened to me when I decided to cooperate with God on this journey of life. My obedience and submission to lie on the altar, along with God using life to tear me down to nothing, put me on the track again. He bandaged my bloodied knees so that I could run the race set before me. I'm determined to fight because I'm determined to win. It's the only option. Who's with me?

DIVINELY MOLDED

"The measure of intelligence is the ability to change."
—ALBERT EINSTEIN[15]

"Everyone thinks of changing the world, but no one thinks of changing himself."
—LEO TOLSTOY[16]

"Change is inevitable; growth is optional."
—JOHN C. MAXWELL[17]

---

15 Thomas Oppong, "Why Albert Einstein Said: The Measure of Intelligence Is the Ability to Change," *The Good Men Project*, 22 Nov. 2020, goodmenproject.com/featured-content/why-albert-einstein-said-the-measure-of-intelligence-is-the-ability-to-change/.

16 Andrea Schlottman, "Leo Tolstoy's Infamous Quote on Changing the World [Quote Graphic]," *Books on the Wall*, 17 May 2018, booksonthewall.com/blog/leo-tolstoy-quote/.

17 John C. Maxwell, *21 Irrefutable Laws of Leadership* (Nashville, TN: Thomas Nelson Inc, 2004).

IF YOU DON'T *FIGHT,* THEN YOU DON'T *WIN*

Frequently, in the Bible, we come across stories of individuals, men and women, who sinned, failed, or just plain blew it. People whom God chose to use, our modern-day churches would excommunicate, create documentaries about, and of course, revoke their ministerial licenses. I get it. Some of these actions and reactions are neither consistent with God's character nor do they represent Him at all, but . . . God met them in the middle of their issues and their messiness, and He still used them greatly.

> **It's so encouraging to me that God takes all of our brokenness, stubbornness, and rebellion and is so patient with us.**

IF YOU DON'T *FIGHT,* THEN YOU DON'T *WIN*

It's so encouraging to me that God takes all of our brokenness, stubbornness, and rebellion and is so patient with us. I'm sure He's in heaven shaking His head every time we think we can do life our own way. Look at King David. What a powerful example of a man who really loved God but who veered off the straight and narrow and was in a place he shouldn't be, looking at what he shouldn't be looking at, doing what he shouldn't do, and then killing Bathsheba's husband to try to cover it all up. That is some 2024 cold-case files stuff. Nothing is new under the sun, right? But it's still encouraging to know we are not alone in the struggle.

What about Noah? If it weren't for Noah, the world as we know it today wouldn't even exist, but good ole Mr. Noah had some trouble with the bottle. What about the apostle Paul? Paul was a Pharisee who persecuted and killed Christians before becoming one himself. Belief Map describes him like this:

> In Galatians 1, Paul said he was famously violent in persecuting Christians "beyond measure." This is an undisputed letter of Paul, and there is no real room for interpreting him otherwise. He exhibits a measure of shame over the matter and is unlikely to be lying. See:
>
> Galatians 1:13-23—For you have heard of my former manner of life in Judaism, how I used to persecute the church of God beyond measure and tried to destroy it; and I was advancing in Judaism beyond many of my contemporaries among my countrymen, being more extremely zealous for my ancestral traditions. . . . I was still unknown by sight to the churches of Judea which

> were in Christ; but only, they kept hearing, "He who once persecuted us is now preaching the faith which he once tried to destroy."[18]

HOWEVER! SOMEBODY SHOUT "HOWEVER!" After Paul's conversion, he is credited for writing almost 25 percent of the New Testament. It literally blows my mind that God delights in taking our mess and turning it into our message.

Another story centers around a woman named Sarah. Sarah, also known as Sarai, had a lot going for her. She was married to a very successful man named Abram, whose name was later changed to Abraham. The thing that caused Sarah to stand out was her exceptional beauty. The Bible describes her as unusually beautiful. We discover in Genesis 11 that she was sixty-five years old yet still considered to be a knock-out! I want her beauty cream. However, with all that Sarah had going for her, there was still one thing missing. One very important thing. Sarah was barren. She did not have children, and for a Jewish woman not to have a child was almost akin to a curse. With all the other great things in her life, Sarah's ability to conceive, gestate, and deliver life was *not* there.

Sarah's physical reality all those years ago is a lot of people's spiritual reality today. You may have a lot going for you. You may be drop-dead gorgeous, born on the right side of the tracks, able to sing like Adele (doubt it), and loaded with lots of money in the bank, but the ability to thrive is absent in your life. The ability to nourish the abundant life that is available by the shed blood

---
18 "Did Paul Violently Persecute Christians?" *BeliefMap.Org*, beliefmap.org/paul/persecuted-christians.

IF YOU DON'T *FIGHT,* THEN YOU DON'T *WIN*

of Jesus is not present in your day to day. YOUR LIFE HAS NO PURPOSE. Have you ever felt like you're just going through the motions? Life is just get up and go to work, pick up the kids, do the laundry, go to bed exhausted with still not enough money in the bank—only to get up and do it again the next day? You're just simply existing, going through the motions: barren.

That was me for many years. In the natural, I had so much going for me: good health, nice looks, a job, a handsome husband, a growing church, and three beautiful, healthy, rambunctious kids, but I was lost with no sense of freedom or purpose. I KNEW that God had called me into ministry, and I was doing that every single day, but I was not experiencing the kingdom, the freedom, or the righteousness, peace, and joy in the Holy Spirit. I was running on empty. Most of you reading this book probably know my story—the one I told in *The Most Beautiful Disaster*—so I won't elaborate, but in 2004, I couldn't run another mile.

> Jesus met me right in the middle of my pain, picked me back up, and held my hand through several years of restoration and showed me a life of purpose, freedom, and joy. I started running again—this time, on a solid foundation.

HOPE CARPENTER

I had crumbled. I had derailed. I was so broken from years and years of anxiety and abuse that I was heartsick and couldn't go another step. I had no idea what to do, so I ran the other way, thinking there must be life out there somewhere. There wasn't, and that only crippled me more until I *really* fell apart in 2013. The good news is this: Jesus met me right in the middle of my pain, picked me back up, held my hand through several years of restoration, and showed me a life of purpose, freedom, and joy. I started running again—this time, on a solid foundation.

Back to Sarah. Today, she would've been an Instagram model and an influencer. She was all that and a bag of (Lay's Salt and Vinegar) chips. It all LOOKED RIGHT. Do you hear me? Abraham and Sarah were Ken and Barbie, Tom and Gisele, Jay-Z and Beyoncé, and maybe even Ron and Hope. God had even promised Abraham that He was going to make his descendants great, the promise of many children. So, Sarah, getting tired of waiting and not trusting the faithfulness of God, turned to the flesh to try to fulfill a spiritual promise. She offered her maidservant, Hagar, to her husband to bear a child for him since she couldn't. Life can do that to us sometimes, can't it? We can reach a point of apparent hopelessness, so much so that we no longer believe that God can or will intervene. Rather than continuing to walk in faith, we begin to take things into our own hands and look for our own solutions. We come up with our own Hagar to try to solve what seems like an impossible situation.

How many of us have believed God for our marriage for so long, and after years of the same old man or the same old woman,

IF YOU DON'T *FIGHT,* THEN YOU DON'T *WIN*

we give up, saying, "They will never change," throw up our hands and move on. How many of us started a business, knowing God told us to, and after a few years of rejection from the bank, having to work around the clock, and being exhausted, we just gave up and walked away only to work in a job that we hated even more than we hated the stress of the business? Sickness, disease that has been diagnosed as "incurable" and we wait, we pray, we confess, and yet we continue to have to take insulin or thyroid medication or lie still for hours during chemotherapy.

I knew a lady who had been single for many years after a terrible marriage that ended in divorce, and she was determined to never settle for "that kind of man" ever again. Days of waiting turned to months, months turned to years, and she found herself still single in her fifties. She was growing very tired and impatient. She turned to online dating, which is fine, but her impatience led her to explore options that she normally wouldn't even consider. She started dating many different men, and, of course, the attention felt great to a very lonely woman. She started going places she would've never gone—clubs, parties, etc.—and was introduced to the "swinger lifestyle."

Now she was a Christian woman who went to church, sang in the choir—all the things. She stopped going to church, went full force into the swinger's party lifestyle, and stayed there for over fifteen years. Eventually, she came into a Sunday service looking like she had aged twenty-five years. She fell into my arms like a heavy, wet blanket; she was a completely broken mess. She came back to the Lord that day, and it was glorious.

It took her some time to gain spiritual strength because of the toll that that type of lifestyle had taken on her.

She's seventy years old now, and God has brought her dream husband into her life. I spoke to her recently, and her regret is that she gave up on God way too soon. She wonders what her life and the many years she wasted because of her impatience and lack of faith would have looked like if she'd remained faithful. Even though she turned to her own "Hagar," God still fulfilled His promise to her in her late years. That's the God we serve.

Listen, if you really want happiness, joy, and fulfillment, if you want to know that you're walking out the purpose and plan of God for your life, don't go "calling looking." Go "God looking." God knows *where* He wants you, WHAT He is calling you to do, *when* He wants you to do it, and HOW it's going to pan out. Therefore, if you want to operate in your purpose, you must be a God-seeker. Seems too simple, right? "It's in HIM that we live and move and have our being" (Acts 17:28, emphasis added). When you find God, His calling will find you. The fruitfulness of the abundant life of God will be experienced out of your relationship with Him. If there is no relationship, you will never walk out the purpose and plan of God for your life.

We get so caught up in chronological time: minutes, hours, days, weeks, months, and years—but God is outside of time, and He sees the big picture when we only see dimly. Our eyes and our focus must be stayed on the One, GOD, who knows the end from the beginning. We must trust that our heavenly Father knows what's best for us and when it's best for us. We

IF YOU DON'T *FIGHT,* THEN YOU DON'T *WIN*

all have times when we get impatient and rebellious and think we know what's best, and that's when we mess up. That's where we veer off the path, the straight and narrow, and think we can do God's job a lot better. How stupid is that? But we all do it. That's when God has to remind us who's in charge and put us on the wheel at the Potter's house.

> **Listen, if you really want happiness, joy, and fulfillment, if you want to know that you're walking out the purpose and plan of God for your life, don't go "calling looking." Go "God looking."**

There are times in the life of every believer when he or she will go through a season of remodeling. It is a time when God strips away old thoughts and habits and replaces them with His truths and principles. Instead of calling it remodeling, I call it the process of brokenness. The prophet Jeremiah describes this so beautifully. It's the story of the potter and the clay. The potter is played by God, and the role of the clay is none other than you and me:

> This is the word that came to Jeremiah from the Lord: "Go down to the potter's house, and there I will give you, my message." So I went down to the potter's house,

> and I saw him working at the wheel. But the pot he was shaping from the clay was marred in his hands; so, the potter formed it into another pot, shaping it as seemed best to him.
>
> Then the word of the Lord came to me. He said, "Can I not do with you, Israel, as this potter does?" declares the Lord. "Like clay in the hand of the potter, so are you in my hand, Israel."—Jeremiah 18:1-6

The moral of the story is this: our life is not our own. Ugh! I hear the screeching and screaming. This is the war of every person's life: releasing control. We want to do what we want to do, whenever we want to do it. Right? Here's the problem with that: only HE knows what we're supposed to do and be. Why? Because He created us, and the problems start when we RESIST the Potter in the molding and the forming, when we want something other than what He's trying to fashion us to be. I know. I know. I ask you again: why do we not trust the character and faithfulness of God in our lives? He's already told us that He has good plans for us, not bad ones. Plans to prosper us (Who doesn't want that?), plans to give us a hope and a future (see Jeremiah 29:11). Yet, we still resist.

When there's a problem with your car, with your laptop, or with your microwave, where do you take it to get fixed? That's right, good answer—the manufacturer. Why don't we take the car to the Apple store? Why don't we take the microwave to the Nissan dealership? We would look foolish if we did that, right? The answer is this: the only person who can fix the issue is the one who made it. God created you, and only God knows

IF YOU DON'T *FIGHT,* THEN YOU DON'T *WIN*

who you were created to be. We do not decide who we will be or what we will do, and the sooner we reconcile this equation, the sooner we will really start living.

> **I'm inviting you to take a trip down to the Potter's house today to be broken and remolded so that you can be what you were created for.**

I'm inviting you to take a trip down to the Potter's house today to be broken and remolded so that you can be what you were created for. Could it be that all the trouble, trials, heartache, misfortune, and pain you've been through was the Potter crushing you—to remake you—because you were resisting His hand in your life? Aren't you tired of living another calendar year miserably trying to hold onto what's not even yours? Like my dear friend I told you about earlier, aren't you tired of wasting years trying to do life your own way only to come back to the manufacturer all beat up and missing parts? Then having to spend time in the "body shop," so to speak, trying to repair all of the broken parts and pieces? Your life is designed by the Potter and must be lived in cooperation with Him so that you can truly live your best life. Stop fighting, and start living.

TROUBLE'S KNOCKING

"By failing to prepare, you are preparing to fail."
—BENJAMIN FRANKLIN[19]

"All things are ready, if our mind be so."
—WILLIAM SHAKESPEARE, HENRY V[20]

---

19 Matt Mayberry, "By Failing to Prepare, You Are Indeed Preparing to Fail," *Entrepreneur*, 22 Apr. 2016, www.entrepreneur.com/leadership/by-failing-to-prepare-you-are-indeed-preparing-to-fail/274494.
20 William Shakespeare, *Henry V* (Overland Park, KS: Digireads, 2017), 4.3.

IF YOU DON'T *FIGHT,* THEN YOU DON'T *WIN*

*H*ave you ever gone to your mailbox, only to find a bill that you weren't expecting? It just showed up mysteriously, and more importantly, it was for an amount that you couldn't pay. Have you been going along your merry way on a merry day and gotten that phone call from your kid's school, telling you that YOUR child was involved in the "smoking in the boys' room" scene? Have you ever been in a relationship, and you thought it was going well? You were anticipating a ring at Christmas, but you got *that* text: "I think we need to take a break. I'm just not feeling this anymore." Sometimes, news just literally comes out of the blue, and you must deal with it right then. It just knocks you off your rocker. You don't have time to prepare for it, pray over it, find a scripture for it, or listen to a podcast from *Ron & Hope Unfiltered* on the subject matter. Trouble is standing at the door.

Let's take a stroll over to King Jehoshaphat's house. In 2 Chronicles 20:17, he received a message from God through Jahaziel, a prophet of the Lord:

IF YOU DON'T *FIGHT,* THEN YOU DON'T *WIN*

> "You will not have to fight this battle. Take up your positions; stand firm and see the deliverance the Lord will give you, Judah, and Jerusalem. Do not be afraid; do not be discouraged. Go out to face them tomorrow, and the Lord will be with you."

The setting for this text was Jehoshaphat being told one morning that they were being attacked. All the "-ites" in the land were planning to make war, and they were only twenty-five miles away. Jehoshaphat had no time to prepare. It was a sneak attack. There was no time to plan a strategy or recruit a mighty army. It came out of nowhere and caught him off guard. So, what did he do? "[King Jehoshaphat] was alarmed but he was resolved" (v. 3). He had the mind within him to go to God. Sometimes, when your back is against the wall, it will show you what you're really made of. Maybe not immediately, but after you lose your mind a minute, it will thrust you into the presence of God like no other time.

Here's the thing about battles and trouble. Sometimes, they will come to your front doorstep—uninvited—as a sneak attack. No time to prepare. This is where your spiritual strength and endurance kick in. This is where you learn what's really inside you and when all those days, weeks, and months of training can kick in. This is when the cream rises to the top. This is when the pure gold shines through. You really don't know what's in you until it's tested.

I used to be a cheerleader in high school, and I loved it. I went to cheer camps and cheer practices, and I cheered in the backyard. I probably could've cheered in my sleep. Well, after high school, I went for many, many years, and I didn't cheer at all. Ron and I started having children in 1994, and we didn't have a little girl until 1998, Chanlin Praise. I was determined that my only girl would be a "girly-girl," but *she* was determined that she would not. She wanted to run in the mud and play baseball with her *"brudders"* (brothers). I put her in dance lessons, gymnastics, and guess what else? Cheerleading. She was still young enough to do it because I said so, so off to cheerleading we went.

> **Here's the thing about battles and trouble.... You really don't know what's in you until it's tested.**

About two practices in, they informed us that the teacher was resigning and asked for parent volunteers. I mean . . . I was a cheerleader, right? I said yes. Do you know that I didn't have to go read a book on cheerleading or watch a YouTube video about cheerleading? I still remembered all the jumps AND their names. I knew the formations and who was a base and who was a flyer based on their abilities. Coaching a cheer team is no traumatic

IF YOU DON'T *FIGHT,* THEN YOU DON'T *WIN*

battle, but the principle still applies. I was prepared because I had spent many years building my endurance and knowledge.

Jehoshaphat's attack came by surprise, and he was outnumbered. But he didn't throw his hands up in defeat at the news of the oncoming attack. What did he do? He did what was natural to him. He went to God. Doing what comes naturally is exactly what each one of us does too. Attacks, trouble, a doctor's report, calls from the school, and surprise break-up texts are coming. The question is this: what is going to be your response? You want the truth? Whatever you are full of is what will come pouring out when the enemy comes poking. The Bible is very clear that whatever is in us will inevitably come out of us. Matthew 12:34-35 (KJV) says this:

> "O generation of vipers, how can ye, being evil, speak good things? for out of the abundance of the heart the mouth speaketh. A good man out of the good treasure of the heart bringeth forth good things: and an evil man out of the evil treasure bringeth forth evil things."

Have you ever been driving down the road, a car just pulls out in front of you, and you blurt out—what? Only you can answer that, and it's either one of two responses: positive—calling on Jesus—or negative—yelling out profanity. What's in us will naturally come out of us. Have you ever been walking through the house, and that little tiny baby toe of yours just jumps in the way of the couch or the table? Yup, me too. What came out of your mouth? I know—it happens to us all. You get the idea, right?

HOPE CARPENTER

Some battles you didn't ask for; they just came to your door or your marriage or your health or your bank account. However, they don't have to knock you out if you're ready to engage them. Jehoshaphat was rattled a bit when he got the news of the sneak attack, but look what he did, or more specifically, look what he prayed:

> "Lord, the God of our ancestors, are you not the God who is in heaven? You rule over all the kingdoms of the nations. Power and might are in your hand, and no one can withstand you. Our God, did you not drive out the inhabitants of this land before your people Israel and give it forever to the descendants of Abraham your friend? They have lived in it and have built in it a sanctuary for your Name, saying, 'If calamity comes upon us, whether the sword of judgment, or plague or famine, we will stand in your presence before this temple that bears your Name and will cry out to you in our distress, and you will hear us and save us.'" —2 Chronicles 20:6-9

Jehoshaphat KNEW where his help came from. This is the text where the worship song came from that states, "It may look like I'm surrounded, but I'm surrounded by you. This is how I fight my battles."[21]

Be like Jehoshaphat. Start reminding God of His faithfulness to you—even if you're not sure what He's doing right now. You might need to remind *yourself* of the faithfulness of God in your life. This is not your first battle, and it won't be your last. This is

---

21 Michael W. Smith, vocalist, "Surrounded (Fight My Battles)," by Elyssa Smith, released February 23, 2018, track 8 on *Surrounded*, Rocketown Records.

not the first time you got a bad report or a break-up letter (text), you wanted to give up and run away from it all, you were hurt, or you didn't have enough in the bank account.

> **Start reminding God of His faithfulness to you—even if you're not sure what He's doing right now. You might need to remind yourself of the faithfulness of God in your life.**

Listen to me right now. It may look like you're surrounded, but we fight differently! Get on your knees, and let faith pour out of you. Instead of saying what you see and feel, why don't you say what God says about your situation and circumstance?

- » God says you are strong, even if you feel weak: "It is God who arms me with strength and keeps my way secure." (Psalm 18:32)
- » God says you are not abandoned, even if you feel alone: "God decided in advance to adopt us into his own family by bringing us to himself through Jesus Christ." (Ephesians 1:5, NLT)
- » God says you are whole and complete, even if you feel fragmented: "So you also are complete through your

union with Christ, who is the head over every ruler and authority." (Colossians 2:10, NLT)
- » God says you are not rejected, but you are His: "Do not fear, for I have redeemed you. I have summoned you by name; you are mine." (Isaiah 43:1)
- » God says you are not alone, even if you feel like you are: "Do not be afraid or discouraged. For the Lord your God is with you wherever you go." (Joshua 1:9)
- » God says you have a purpose and a good life ahead of you, even when you can't see it: "For I know the plans I have for you, declares the Lord, plans for good and not for evil, to give you a future and a hope." (Jeremiah 29:11, author paraphrase)

Do I need to go on? I could. I can do this *all* day. Listen to me. When you are in a battle that snuck into your life, that caught you by surprise, you still must fight. However, you have to fight differently. *What does that mean, Hope?* I'm glad you asked.

Let's go back to 2 Chronicles 20:12: "Our God, will you not judge them? For we have no power to face this vast army that is attacking us. We do not know what to do, but our eyes are on you." Oh, my goodness. Did you hear that? "We do NOT know what to do, but our eyes are on the problem, our eyes are on the doctors' reports, our eyes are on the negative numbers in the bank account, our eyes are on the police report." Absolutely not! But OUR EYES ARE ON YOU LORD! There are just some battles that are way too big for us. There are situations in our

IF YOU DON'T *FIGHT,* THEN YOU DON'T *WIN*

lives that come to take us out, but if we keep our eyes on our God, He will fight for us.

> **There are just some battles that are way too big for us. There are situations in our lives that come to take us out, but if we keep our eyes on our God, He will fight for us.**

When I was in elementary school, there was a boy who was just a full-blown bully, and he loved to pick on the girls—for whatever reason. Well, in second grade, I was his punching bag. I remember walking into school. I didn't even want to make eye contact with him because I knew what was coming. I probably didn't weigh fifty pounds soaking wet, even in second grade (those were the days), so I was an easy target. Well, after about three weeks of this bullying, I'd had enough. I went home and told my brother Jody who was five years older than me.

Jody proceeded to walk me to my classroom the next day, and when, let's call him Keith, started running his mouth about how skinny my legs were, Jody took over. I didn't have to say a word. I didn't need to cry. I just stood there and watched my *big brother* handle this situation FOR me. Jody looked down at this little guy and proceeded to tell him that if he was going to mess with me, then he was going to have to deal with Jody. And do you know, from that day forward, I never dealt with Keith again.

I need you to know that when you have a battle that is just too big for you, you have an "Older Brother" who is way bigger and much stronger than any enemy you are facing. Just *stand still*, keep your eyes on Jesus, and watch him fight for you. You won't lose the battle if you don't lose your focus. Stop allowing the problems to get all your attention so that you're blinded to the power and might of our great God. He has never, even one time, left you or forsaken you, and He won't start now.

There is resurrection power inside of you that wants to come out, but you have to keep your eyes fixed on the One who started the process in you and who will be faithful to complete the process in you: "Looking to Jesus the author and finisher of our faith: who for the joy set before him endured the cross, despising the shame, and is set down at the right hand of the throne of God" (Hebrews 12:2, author paraphrase). Just like Jesus, there will be battles that we just have to endure because we know that there is a prize on the other side of our pain. Our eyes must be fixed on HIM; He is our goal. He is why we run this race, and we are called to run with endurance.

What does it mean to be focused? When we focus, we give a lot of attention to one thing. ONE THING. I don't know about you, but it is very difficult for me to be laser-focused on just one thing, especially if there are a lot of things in my life that need

IF YOU DON'T *FIGHT,* THEN YOU DON'T *WIN*

attention. I remember when our kids were younger (and we had three under the age of four). It seemed like there was never enough time in the day to get everything done that needed to be done: The endless amounts of dirty clothes that needed to be washed, dried, folded, AND put away because if they weren't put away, one of these little kids who was running around the house was going to make them part of their playtime.

What about three square meals a day, not to mention bottles, formula, dishes, and dirty diapers? I used to be so happy to get the bed sheets changed. The thought of lying down at night, being so exhausted, on clean sheets was heavenly . . . only to wake up the next day with one of the three having an "oops" on the clean sheets. There is just so much to take care of when the kids are little. Then, school starts. There's homework, ball practice, ball games, dance lessons, choir practice, school projects, and field trips, and the to-do list at home with laundry and yardwork is still there. Oh, and I have a spouse. I almost forgot about Ronald! And isn't that what we do? There's so much to do that we sometimes forget the most important things.

Romans 8:28-30 (NKJV) tells us this:

> And we know that all things work together for good to those who love God, to those who are called according to His purpose. [Keep reading. He's not done yet.] For whom He foreknew, He also predestined to be conformed to the image of His Son [GOAL] . . . Moreover whom He predestined, these He also called; whom He called, these He also justified; and whom He justified, these He also glorified.

This is ALL IN PAST TENSE! God sees you finished, a finished product. All things work together . . . knowing this . . . He already knew me (foreknew me), and the goal is that I'm predestined to look like Jesus. I'm called and chosen, justified and glorified. All of this is good news. There is nothing to hang our heads and mope around about in these scriptures. Sounds to me that your life and mine are already planned out, and no matter what happens, good or bad, it all works out in the end for those of us who love God and who are called according to His PURPOSE. God chose you when your past was still in the future! Whew-wee—that makes me want to throw a party over here! God loves you, and your past is a part of the equation. God has finished the book of your life and works backward. Why? So that He can make all things work together for your good.

> I think we get it twisted and start to aim toward success instead of significance—a life that fulfills God's purpose and plans, not ours. The life we are called to is an upward call.

Isaiah 46:10 declares, "I make known the end from the beginning, from ancient times, what is still to come. I say,

IF YOU DON'T *FIGHT,* THEN YOU DON'T *WIN*

'My purpose will stand, and I will do all that I please.'" We first must be convinced that God has a good plan for us and keep our eyes set on Him so that we can run this race with endurance. We won't run hard toward a life that does not get us excited about the future. What are you chasing anyway? Is it a big bank account? Thousands of followers on social media? "Boss" status?

I think we get it twisted and start to aim toward *success* instead of *significance*—a life that fulfills God's purpose and plans, not ours. The *life* we are called to is an upward call. Philippians 3:13-14 (KJV) says this:

> Brethren, I count not myself to have apprehended: but this one thing I do, forgetting those things which are behind, and reaching forth unto those things which are before, I press toward the mark for the prize of the high calling of God in Christ Jesus.

That's it! Are we striving to live the *good* life that is filled with prominence, fame, large bank accounts, and luxury? We should be striving to live the *blessed* life in God that is a calling that brings significance rather than success by way of the world's standards. If God has called you to live in a hut in Haiti serving as a missionary without the modern luxuries of the world, you can still live a full, happy life. How? Because you are walking out your calling and purpose. You are living according to PURPOSE. If you are working ninety hours a week with barely enough time to do your own laundry, but it's the life God called you to, you will be at peace and fulfilled. Purpose. Calling.

This is what drives us and keeps us on the upward path, even if the path is steep and rocky. The goal is to finish the race and win, but you won't run hard, and you won't run long if there is nothing calling you at the finish line.

Let's talk a bit more about this race. Hebrews 12:1-2 says this:

> Therefore, since we are surrounded by such a great cloud of witnesses, let us throw off everything that hinders and the sin that so easily entangles. And let us run with perseverance the race marked out for us. Fixing our eyes on Jesus, the pioneer and perfecter of faith. For the joy set before Him he endured the cross, scorning its shame and sat down at the right hand of the throne of God.

So I've already stated all of the things life is overwhelming us with—all of the to-dos in our lives that seem to keep us scattered and unfocused, but then there's this Scripture that urges us to throw off the sin that entangles us and the things that so easily hinder us so that we can set our eyes on Jesus. Ahh . . . this is a recipe for success! This is the recipe for running our race and ending well. Nowhere in this Scripture does it say that if we focus on Jesus that all the merry maids will show up in the middle of the night to do our laundry and yard work, does it? It does say that we still must persevere in our run, but the prize in front of us keeps us running. We will have to figure out what hinders us, identify the sin in our lives that keeps us tangled up, and then deal with that sin. We've got our fair share

IF YOU DON'T *FIGHT,* THEN YOU DON'T *WIN*

of work to do, but our focus must be adjusted so that we can run and keep running.

My question for you today is this: What are you focusing on? What or who has your attention? Is your focus on the condition of your home? The lack of resources in your bank account? Your lack of education? All the mistakes you've made until now that seem to have you stuck? The heartbreaks and back stabs that make you cautious to try again? Yes, some of these things do require our attention, but they cannot be our primary focus, or they will consume our hearts and minds and cause us to doubt our good God who has already planned a good life for us. Focusing on all that is wrong in our lives will cause us to sink into self-pity and bitterness and ultimately drown out the fervor and life of God. What we focus on, we become.

> **What we focus on, we become.**

Another important aspect of that Scripture in Hebrews 12 is the phrase "run with perseverance or endurance." Endurance is steadfastness as God enables the believer to remain (endure) under the challenges of life. Only with our eyes on the prize, Jesus, will we be able to run with all the challenges of life being thrown in our path. I've never been a runner (shocker, right?), but I do know some people who love to run, jog, and even do marathons. Why? I do not know, but I know enough about the sport to be able to talk about it considering this Scripture.

To build endurance for a long run, you first must evaluate your fitness for the task at hand. Endurance training is a thing, and it describes the following:

> Any type of athletic training that increases your body's cardiovascular or muscular endurance. Endurance training helps develop the body's respiratory capabilities and muscular strength to sustain physical activity with lower injury risks for extended periods.[22]

Runners and cyclists use distance training to develop overall endurance. It requires an athlete to achieve a specific distance goal, such as running five miles or swimming one mile. Runners may choose to do this on pavement or trails, and cyclists may use treadmills or exercise bikes. There are other types of endurance training that can be used, such as tempo, circuit, strength, and interval training. The goal is to become stronger, increasing endurance so that you can run longer at a better speed. To do this, you must fuel your body, choose the type of training, measure your actual performance, rest, increase difficulty, remeasure your performance, and then remain consistent.

You can't just feed your body any old thing when you are trying to build endurance. You can't be a couch potato and binge on Netflix. You must be honest with yourself about yourself. There are days that rest is the only goal so that you can

---

[22] "Endurance Training: How to Increase Endurance – 2023," *MasterClass*, 12 Jan. 2022, www.masterclass.com/articles/endurance-training-explained#.

IF YOU DON'T *FIGHT,* THEN YOU DON'T *WIN*

tackle tomorrow. There will be days that are just harder than others, but we can't quit when the pressure's on. If you will delete those subscriptions that you are feeding on that are doing nothing but weakening your spirit and start feeding on the Word of God every day, get up and go to church or a life group to have good, healthy, godly connections that are life-giving, and then be honest about where you are in this race of life, resting if you need to, but never quitting, you will run, and you will run well. Pressure builds endurance *if* you don't let the pressure crush you. You can win, but you must press for it; press toward the mark of the high call of God in Christ.

> **Trouble will always be a part of the journey, but the enemy has a way of amplifying the trouble in your mind to make you think it's bigger than it really is.**

Listen to me right now. Trouble will always be a part of the journey, but the enemy has a way of amplifying the trouble in your mind to make you think it's bigger than it really is. Even when you see adversity, you must be steady and run with endurance. When pain hits your body, your kids are acting crazy, your husband doesn't come home, money is low in the bank, and your enemies are everywhere, be steady and keep going. You have to run when they don't like you. You have to run when you're tired. You have to run when you're worried. You have to run when you're mad. The storm that is all around you will not take you out IF you keep your eyes fixed straight ahead on Jesus, the prize. Don't take your eyes off of Jesus.

Remember that God has said this:

> When you pass through the waters, I will be with you; and when you pass through the rivers, they will not sweep over you. When you walk through the fire, you will not be burned; the flames will not set you ablaze. —Isaiah 43:2

There will be raging waters and deep rivers along the journey, but God has promised to be with you and not let you drown. Sometimes, God delivers you from the furnace, but other times, He holds your hand in the furnace, knowing what it will produce in you. Trouble is not authorized to consume you and destroy you; it is authorized to make you into something. Pain produces in our lives if we let it. There is a predestined good life already chosen for you, but you must run toward it with your eyes fixed on Jesus, the author and finisher of this run (your faith).

The stronger I am spiritually, the more power I can generate and the longer I can run. Speed is built on a foundation of endurance—what I can endure and the weight I can bear. Ahh . . . so trials and pain are there to strengthen me, not crush me. Think about all the trials and pain that you've had to endure in your life. Just stop a minute and think about them. I bet most of us would say that there have been many things we have gone through that have, indeed, strengthened us, things that we overcame and "got through", but there are other things that have really hindered us and caused so much damage. It's those things that have slowed us down or maybe even caused us to lay on the ground with blood running down our knees. Those things that are still bleeding are the things that we haven't learned from and have chosen to let them fester like a cancer that is slowly eating us alive. Trials and hard things are all a part of life; the key to surviving them is a strong foundation on the Lord.

Our relationship with the Lord is our only hope of surviving the storms of life—and not just surviving but coming out stronger, better, and wiser. If you want to win in this race called life, you must run toward your called purpose with your eyes on Jesus, allowing the pressure to strengthen you and not destroy you. The choice is yours.

Our relationship with the Lord is our only hope of surviving the storms of life—and not just surviving but coming out stronger, better, and wiser.

HOW'S YOUR HEART?

"Whatever does not kill me makes me stronger."
—FRIEDRICH NIETZSCHE[23]

"Failure is only the opportunity to begin again, this time more intelligently."
—HENRY FORD[24]

"There is no better than adversity. Every defeat, every heartbreak, every loss, contains its own seed, its own lesson on how to improve your performance the next time."
—MALCOLM X[25]

---

23 Friedrich Wilhelm Nietzsche, et al. *Twilight of the Idols and the Anti-Christ* (Overland Park, KS: Digireads, 2018).
24 Henry Ford, *My Life and Work* (Garden City, NY: Garden City Publishing, 1922) 19.
25 "Malcolm X: Children, Assassination & Quotes," *History.Com*, 2 Nov. 2022, www.history.com/topics/black-history/malcolm-x.

IF YOU DON'T *FIGHT,* THEN YOU DON'T *WIN*

The title of this book is *If You Don't Fight, Then You Don't Win*. Win what? What on earth are we trying to win? Is it a bigger house? A better position at work? A tall, dark, and handsome hubby? Early retirement? What am I even talking about when I say that?

Our goal is to see Jesus and live with Him eternally, but we also have a goal here on earth to become more like Jesus and to live this amazing, abundant life that we're promised. We will not finish well and operate in kingdom living here on earth if we are not pursuing wholeness. Too many Christians choose to live in bitterness, unforgiveness, strife, jealousy, negative attitudes, and stinking thinking, and it causes us to stumble on the track of life as we're running. Trials and pain do not discriminate, but if we don't deal with the bitterness and pain that we are carrying, our hearts will not be strong enough to run while living our best life. We will derail, fall apart, and live a miserable life, even though an amazing life is available to us all. So, we must first get our hearts cleaned and healed so that we are strong enough to run.

IF YOU DON'T *FIGHT,* THEN YOU DON'T *WIN*

> **The problem with pain is that life moves so fast that we just tend to sweep it under the rug and keep stepping.... The truth is, the pain is sinking into the soil of our hearts, and it is germinating, growing, and producing a harvest in our lives.**

Hebrews 12 describes this posture in running our race as "things that hinder and the sin that so easily entangles us." Another confirmation is that in our lives, we will have "things" that keep us from running well to obtain the promises of God in our lives. That passage of scripture shows Jesus running His own race on earth: "For the joy set before him, he endured the cross, scorning its shame, and sat down at the right hand of the throne of God" (Hebrews 12:2). Jesus did not want to go to the cross, but He understood that the pain of the cross was a vital part of the process of obtaining the prize. And what was the great prize? You and me. A family. This scripture is so powerful to me because it reminds me that my victory is my responsibility, and it gives me step-by-step instructions on how to run to win. We have to know the things in our own lives that are hindering us and weighing us down from running at top speed, with endurance, and we also have to be really honest about our sins and issues that keep tripping us up. Each of us will have our own set of "things", our own weaknesses, and our own bloodline sins that we all must deal with (not overlook or sweep under the rug), so that we win our own race. Sin and weights bring residual effects into our lives like bitterness, unforgiveness, generational sins, physical illnesses, depression and anxiety, and the inability to sustain healthy relationships, and they MUST be dealt with to be able to run well.

The problem with pain and unresolved issues in our lives is that life moves so fast that we just tend to sweep it under the rug and keep stepping. We say things like, "I'll be okay," or "I'll get over it," and the truth is, the pain is sinking into the soil of our hearts, and it is germinating, growing, and producing a harvest in our lives. What about the roots? The roots are getting bigger and stronger, and the longer we wait to deal with the hurt and pain, the harder it is to pull it up out of our hearts. We must first be willing to examine who we are and why we do what we do to be able to start the process of digging up and cleaning out our hearts. Most people don't get better in life because they just don't take the time to search their souls and ask the hard questions. We keep our heads in the sand and think life should just turn out better. This is just flawed thinking. If you want life to be better, then do something to make it better. Start with you—your heart.

I mentioned earlier that I grew up in a little town in South Carolina—Calhoun Falls—and it was a very simple life. My parents went to the same jobs throughout my childhood. They would come home, my mom would cook, and my dad would

IF YOU DON'T *FIGHT*, THEN YOU DON'T *WIN*

do yardwork or piddle in the garage on some antique piece of furniture. Saturday was a workday for us all, and spring and summer brought the most dreaded chore in the world: pulling weeds. I hated pulling weeds, but here is the thing about weeds. If you pull them when they are young and fresh, they are so easy to pluck out of the ground. If you wait several days, or, Lord forbid, weeks, then it's very difficult to get them out of the ground. If you totally neglect them, then you will be overpowered by them, and total reconstruction in the yard is needed to clean them out.

The same principle applies to the weeds in our hearts. The weeds in our hearts are all the issues of life: rape, divorce, abuse, lack of unconditional love, negative words spoken about us and over us, sinful habits, lifestyles, and so on. The bottom line is this: pain produces a terrible harvest in our lives. If we want to run this race well (run to win), then we must take the time to address the issues in our hearts. If we keep trying to run when we're heartsick, we will eventually collapse. That's exactly what happened to me.

I went into adulthood with so many weeds of pain and trauma in my heart. I thought that just changing my last name and my address would make everything go away. It didn't. I never dealt with any of the abuse, the rape, the constant fighting and turmoil in my home as a child, the lies that I had taken to be the truth about myself, and the masks that I wore that had become so normal to me, and then I was thrown into ministry where I felt I *couldn't* expose any of that for fear of rejection. After all, I wasn't "perfect."

HOPE CARPENTER

I continued to run for fifteen years into marriage until my heart and mind collapsed when I was thirty-five years old. I won't go into the whole story because I already wrote a book about that—*The Most Beautiful Disaster*. If you haven't read it, you need to, especially if this chapter is speaking loudly to you. I know the weight of trying to do life well when one is not well. Those two concepts don't mix. They're like oil and water. I said all that to say this: if you've experienced a traumatic life or the enemy has tainted your past, you must take the time to deal with all those weeds that have taken up permanent residence in your heart. They aren't ever going away on their own. They're growing and becoming stronger, and the longer you wait, the harder it will be to uproot them.

There is a medical term called debridement:

> Debridement is a procedure for treating a wound in the skin. It involves thoroughly cleaning the wound and removing all hyperkeratotic (thickened skin or callus), infected, and nonviable (necrotic or dead) tissue, foreign debris, and residual material from dressings. Debridement can be accomplished either surgically or through alternate methods such as use of special dressings and gels.[26]

Merriam-Webster defines debridement as "usually surgical removal of lacerated, devitalized, or contaminated tissue from a wound." My mom and sister-in-law are nurses, and they will

---

[26] Rob Mayfield, "Debridement," *University of California San Francisco Department of Surgery*, surgery.ucsf.edu/conditions—procedures/debridement.aspx.

IF YOU DON'T *FIGHT,* THEN YOU DON'T *WIN*

concur that caring for a wound can be complicated. The healing process can be slow and tedious, and much oversight is needed. If any unhealthy tissue remains, then debridement is necessary *so that* the healing process can take place. When our hearts are not cleared of the effects of the painful, unhealthy events in our lives, we will walk around sick and broken, unable to experience the abundant life of God. IT IS IMPERATIVE that we stop, step off the track of life, lie on the operating table, allow the Lord to examine our hearts, and then rid them of the pain we've been carrying so that we can heal and gain our strength to be ready to run again.

> **IT IS IMPERATIVE that we stop, step off the track of life, lie on the operating table, allow the Lord to examine our hearts, and then rid them of the pain we've been carrying so that we can heal and gain our strength to be ready to run again.**

Hope, how do I do this? I know I need to, but I don't even know where to start. You're starting right now. Do you feel that pain in your chest? The lump in your throat? Maybe warm tears are streaming down your face right now. That is you allowing your heart to breathe, but there's so much more work to be done. Or maybe you're the one with the high pain tolerance, and you're clenching your teeth tight, not allowing yourself to feel at all. If that's you, you can keep doing what you're doing, but you will do exactly that. You will circle the same mountain, view the same scenery, and stay stuck.

I am not one of those people who blame everything on the way I was raised or all the negative things that I've gone through in life. I do believe that all the things I've been through have affected me, and if I choose to wallow in the pain of the past, my life will remain stuck and stagnant, reeking of the pain from yesterday. Listen. The past is gone. No matter how hard you try, you cannot change one thing that has happened to you or that you've done. If you linger there, you will always live in regret, stay in depression, feel miserable, and be miserable to be around. Living in the past handicaps your ability to have an amazing present and be hopeful for the future. Deal with the pain from the past, grieve the losses, seal it in the coffin, throw the dirt over it, dry the tears, forgive whom you need to, and move on. Keep moving forward. This is called *grow through what you go through*, and it's the act of facing the pain and obstacles in our lives and overcoming them. Let them be *fuel* for your next season rather than cyanide.

My rock-bottom year was 2013, and boy, did I take a spectacular fall. At that point, I looked at the crumbled pieces of my broken life and wondered how on earth I would ever be able to make anything out of the mess. It seemed too big, too public,

IF YOU DON'T *FIGHT*, THEN YOU DON'T *WIN*

too overwhelming, and too much to deal with, but I really only had two choices: stay in my brokenness or try to rebuild stronger. I chose the latter, and here I am today, writing my third book, leading a mentorship ministry with hundreds of people in it, traveling all over the world, sharing the good news of the gospel, and living my best life yet. I dedicated several years to debridement, cleaning out the wounds, and replacing the old patterns of thinking and doing life with new patterns of discipline, structure, and accountability. I had to address issues all the way back to my childhood, teenage years, early marriage, and my awful season of "lostness."

This was not quick, and it surely wasn't easy, but I knew that it was possible—if I would put in the work. I refused to let the pain of my early years and even the pain of my downfall dictate my future. I had to embrace the reality that a life of staying free would require work on a daily basis. After the emergency room experience of the crash of my life and the critical care room I had to stay in for many months, I moved into a regular routine of staying whole and free and it looks a bit like this.

Letting go of pain is a life-long process of addressing the issues one at a time; it's like peeling the skin from an onion. It's a daily habit of examining your heart.

HOPE CARPENTER

Letting go of pain is a life-long process of addressing the issues one at a time; it's like peeling the skin from an onion. It's a daily habit of examining your heart. I do it each night before I go to bed and the reason I do it is found in Ephesians 4:26 (NLV), "If you are angry, do not let it become sin. Get over your anger before the day is finished." I ask the Lord to show me where I was offended, hurt, or angered that day, and I write it down in my journal. Then I ask forgiveness for my sinful response to the pain, whether it was anger, unforgiveness, or whatever. That process quickly and easily plucks the weeds out of my heart so that they won't produce a bad harvest in my life. Then I ask the Lord to teach me whatever it is that I need to learn from the pain. *What do you mean, Hope?* Nothing is ever wasted in our lives. Romans 8:28 tells us that "all things work together [produce] for our good." It didn't say that all things *are* good. Instead, the good and the bad work together and end up producing good.

I've had to cook all my life, and I understand ingredients and what it takes to produce food that tastes good. In baking a yummy, delicious cake, you must put some yucky things in there too. None of us would go get a cup of flour and eat JUST THAT for dinner, right? What about a stick of butter alone? Nope, not that either. What about a tablespoon of salt or cinnamon? Gross. No way. But add all of that together and put it in the oven under the heat (that's another chapter in itself), and man, oh man, it's amazing! It's the same with our lives. If you allow the Master Builder, the Master Baker, our heavenly Father,

IF YOU DON'T *FIGHT,* THEN YOU DON'T *WIN*

to use all the "stuff" in our lives and mix it all up and trust the process, He will make it all work together for good.

I believe that I am speaking prophetically to you right now, and the Word of the Lord for YOU is: IT'S TIME TO GET UP. Sometimes we are so bruised and broken that our spirit is slumbering, barely breathing, like walking, talking, dead men. We have been beaten until we are barely conscious, disappointment after disappointment, to the point that we are reeling in depression, and at this moment we need shock therapy. I'm the ER doctor right now holding the defibrillator over your heart and I'm screaming at the top of my lungs in your face, "WAKE UP, DON'T GIVE UP NOW, THERE'S SO MUCH MORE TO LIVE FOR." When Jesus healed people, He would tell them to "arise, get up." To the paralytic, Jesus told him to get up, pick up your mat and walk (see John 5:8). It's so interesting to me that Jesus commanded him to operate in the very thing that was wrong in his life. His legs were paralyzed but Jesus told him to walk. Jesus said to Jairus's daughter, "Little girl, I say to you get up" (Mark 5:41). Getting up to pursue this great life that is available to us can seem so overwhelming, especially when you're exhausted from battle and you're looking around the ashes of your life with sweat on your brow and blood streaming down your face. You *know* that THIS isn't the "good life" God has called you to, but the actual good life will require so much work and you're just not sure if you have it in you. I call that miserably secure and living the miserable life of misery is a death sentence. You're dying on the table right now, and I'm here throwing you a lifeline. I'm using all I have to help you live, but you must muster up the will to wake up.

Pain can keep you bound up and weighted down to the point you can't run at all. You must take the time to debride the pain from your heart and then take more time to heal and recover. Do a heart check daily so that the weeds don't creep in and overtake you. Allow the Lord to use any and everything that touches your life and weave it into your story so that it no longer holds you down, but becomes fuel for your race. It really is true: *what doesn't kill you makes you stronger if you let it.*

FIGHT THE GOOD FIGHT OF FAITH

"Life keeps throwing me stones. And I keep finding the diamonds."
—ANA CLAUDIA ANTUNES

"Show me someone who has done something worthwhile, and I'll show you someone who has overcome adversity."
— LOU HOLTZ

IF YOU DON'T *FIGHT,* THEN YOU DON'T *WIN*

Fighting to become who you were originally created to be shouldn't be an option. It can't be an option. You should want that bad enough, but as we've discussed in previous chapters, sometimes, we are too weak and need time to heal before we put the boxing gloves on, right? But the truth is this: there's always something to fight, whether it's our own minds, our insecurities, the business of life, or fighting to be everything we were created to be. Pick your hard. We also talked about that in chapter 3.

Sinking into the mundane mindset of mediocrity is so much easier than staring at the worst case scenario and telling it NO! That takes courage and grit.

IF YOU DON'T *FIGHT*, THEN YOU DON'T *WIN*

Sinking into the mundane mindset of mediocrity is so much easier than staring at the worst case scenario and telling it NO! That takes courage and grit. Dharius Daniels, a wonderful friend and co-laborer, says it so well in his book *Your Purpose is Calling*: "You and I can easily catch sickness, but we will never catch health. Sickness is passive, just like mediocrity. But health is active, just like excellence. It requires effort."[27] Just like we don't catch health, we don't catch becoming great or walking out our divine purpose; we have to fight for that.

Okay, Dharius. Okay, Hope. I hear you, but what does that look like? Hebrews 6:12 tells us, "We do not want you to become lazy, but to imitate those who through faith and patience inherit what has been promised." Faith and patience are the instructions here for us to run this race and fight this fight, so let's dive into them. Fiction writers have a rule: "Show. Don't tell," and that's exactly what the writer of Hebrews did for us in the Hall of Faith. He declared that "without faith, it is impossible to please God" (Hebrews 11:6), and then he went on to give us many examples of the faith-filled lives of the people recorded in the Bible, the adversity they overcame, and how they did it by faith!

Catch this:

> Now faith is confidence in what we hope for and assurance about what we do not see. This is what the ancients were commended for.

---

[27] Dharius Daniels, *Your Purpose Is Calling: Your Difference Is Your Destiny* (Grand Rapids, MI: Zondervan Books, 2022) 143.

HOPE CARPENTER

By faith we understand that the universe was formed at God's command, so that what is seen was not made out of what was visible.

By faith Abel brought God a better offering than Cain did. By faith he was commended as righteous, when God spoke well of his offerings. And by faith Abel still speaks, even though he is dead.

By faith Enoch was taken from this life, so that he did not experience death: "He could not be found, because God had taken him away." For before he was taken, he was commended as one who pleased God. And without faith it is impossible to please God, because anyone who comes to him must believe that he exists and that he rewards those who earnestly seek him.

By faith Noah, when warned about things not yet seen, in holy fear built an ark to save his family. By his faith he condemned the world and became heir of the righteousness that is in keeping with faith.

By faith Abraham, when called to go to a place he would later receive as his inheritance, obeyed and went, even though he did not know where he was going. By faith he made his home in the promised land like a stranger in a foreign country; he lived in tents, as did Isaac and Jacob, who were heirs with him of the same promise. For he was looking forward to the city with foundations, whose architect and builder is God. And by faith even Sarah, who was past childbearing age, was enabled to bear children because she considered him faithful who had made the promise. And so from this one man, and he as good as dead, came descendants as numerous as the stars in the sky and as countless as the sand on the seashore.—Hebrews 11:1-17

IF YOU DON'T *FIGHT,* THEN YOU DON'T *WIN*

Hebrews 11 is chock-full of "show-don't-tell" examples of how we are to live this life by faith so that we inherit the promises of God. Clearly, we will have to constantly fight this good fight daily to be able to overcome. I think that's the part of Christian living that most people do not want to embrace—the fact that it's work.

Some think that once they get saved, only good things happen, and God doesn't or shouldn't allow anything other than that. The moment we accept and embrace that hardship, pain, and enduring to the end are parts of this race, the easier the race gets. You won't be so blindsided when you understand that you have an enemy who hates you and is constantly trying to bombard you with sucker punches. Our job is to keep our eyes fixed on Jesus, say what God says, and not be distracted by what we see, feel, and hear.

> **The moment we accept and embrace that hardship, pain, and enduring to the end are parts of this race, the easier the race gets.**

My definition of faith is looking at nothing and calling it something. Looking at the facts around us but responding to the facts with the truth of God's Word and what He's already provided for me. *That*, my friend, is work—a fight, but it's a good fight that produces a great harvest in our lives. We have to learn how to respond to tests and battles the way Jesus did. Jesus didn't have an emotional response to Satan when he came tempting, threatening, and accusing; He just responded with truth—with God's Word. Jesus didn't freak out, backslide, cut somebody, or cuss; He just spoke truth.

Truth changes facts all day long, according to the apostle Paul:

> This know also, that in the last days perilous times shall come. For men shall be lovers of their own selves, covetous, boasters, proud, blasphemers, disobedient to parents, unthankful, unholy, without natural affection, trucebreakers, false accusers, incontinent, fierce, despisers of those that are good, traitors, heady, high-minded, lovers of pleasures more than lovers of God; having a form of godliness, but denying the power thereof: from such turn away. For of this sort are they which creep into houses, and lead captive silly women laden with sins, led away with divers lusts, ever learning, AND NEVER ABLE TO COME TO THE KNOWLEDGE OF THE TRUTH.—2 Timothy 3:1-7 (KJV, emphasis added)

This mindset has plagued the body of Christ for ages and still does today when people's lives never line up with the truth they've heard. We can hear it, recite it, and have it taped to the refrigerator, but if it's not embraced and walked out, it has no impact. It is possible to believe a truth but never see the reality of it in our own lives, but the only part of the Word that we will experience

IF YOU DON'T *FIGHT,* THEN YOU DON'T *WIN*

is the part we lay hold of. We will not enjoy and live out what belongs to us; we will only occupy what we put a demand on.

To overcome and operate like Jesus did we have to be filled through and through, so the enemy can have no place in us. God wants to occupy space in us, and Jesus is our example. When the enemy came to Jesus, He said, "You have no place in me" (John 14:30), and God wants our response to be the same when we are faced with the battles in our lives: "Satan, I'm so full of God. You have no space in me." Now, here's the patience part: John 15:4, depending on the version you read, says, "Remain [abide] in me and I will remain [abide] in you." And John 15:7-8 (KJV) says the following:

> "If ye abide in me, and my words abide in you, ye shall ask what ye will, and it shall be done unto you. Herein is my Father glorified, that ye bear much fruit; so shall ye be my disciples."

This is the only way we can stand sure-footed in the face of the enemy when all hell is coming against us and that is to know the truth and remain in it. This is how we get our prayers answered! Saying what God says instead of what we see. ("If you abide in me and my words abide in you, you shall ask what you will, and it shall be done unto you.") Guys, this is God's Word and His only Word. This is not my opinion or a self-help class. Let's keep reading in John to get a deeper revelation of the benefits of abiding (staying and being patient) in Him: John 15:9-11 (emphasis added) says,

HOPE CARPENTER

> "Now remain in my love. If you keep my commands, you will remain in my love, just as I have kept my Father's commands and remain in his love. I have told you this so that my joy may be in you and that your joy may be COMPLETE."

Oh, my goodness. Did you hear that? We can have complete joy in the midst of suffering all because we've been faithful, consistent abiders in Him. This is gold right here. God gave to every one of His children a measure of faith, the God-kind of faith, and when we speak and operate in this kind of faith, we hold the door open for God to do the work for us, and hard things become light. *Huh? Light and easy?* Yes, ma'am and yes, sir:

> And this small and temporary trouble we suffer will bring us a tremendous and eternal glory, much greater than the trouble. For we fix our attention, not on things that are seen, but on things that are unseen. What can be seen lasts only for a time, but what cannot be seen lasts forever.—2 Corinthians 4:17-18 (GNT)

Wow. You must stop looking at what you're going through and embrace what it is going to produce in your life. Jesus knew that going to the cross was going to be hard, awful, painful, and unjust, and He did not want to go, but He said, "There's joy on the other side of the cross" (Hebrews 12:2, author paraphrase). The prize was worth the process, and so is this fight of faith for you and me. A man of faith calls hard things light and easy, but a man of feeling calls it hard and heavy. A man of feeling, a temporal man, can't see what's on the other side of pain, but a man of faith looks at nothing and calls it something.

> **The prescription for every trial is the Word of God, and you must know the Word of God. God's Word is your weapon against the enemy.**

The prescription for every trial is the Word of God, and you *must* know the Word of God. God's Word is your weapon against the enemy. It will shut him up, make him tuck his tail, and run in the other direction. God's Word is our hope, and we are comforted in times of trouble by God's Word. His Word holds our miracles. His Word gets us through the dark places: "His word is a lamp to my feet and a light to my path," Psalm 119:105 (author paraphrase). God sent His Word and healed us, according to Psalm 107:20. There's no way we can live victoriously without the Word of God.

I want to encourage you to get into the Word. If you never read another book again, make His Word your priority. It is EVERYTHING:
- » It's life and peace. (John 6:63)
- » It helps us know God. (Proverbs 2:1-5)

- » It's a weapon. (Hebrews 4:12)
- » It's comfort. (Psalm 119:50)
- » It shines light on darkness. (Psalm 119:105)
- » It makes the enemy flee. (Ephesians 6:17, Revelation 12:11)
- » It washes our mind of old ways of thinking. (John 17:17, Romans 12:1, Hebrews 4:12)
- » It keeps us from sinning. (Psalm 119:11)
- » It's our guide. (Psalm 119:105 and 133)
- » It's our source of faith. (Romans 10:17)
- » It revives and strengthens us. (Psalm 119:25, 50, and 114)
- » It heals us. (Proverbs 4:22)

God's Word works if you work the Word. News flash! NO ONE'S COMING TO SAVE YOU! Only you can fight your battles, and only your voice can remove your mountains. Your parents' faith can't move *your* mountains. Your spouse's faith can't move *your* mountains. You are responsible for you. If you're going to be successful, *you* will make it happen. If you're going to live in peace, *you* will make it happen. If you're going to walk out the promises of God, *you* will have to fight for them. If you give up because you're tired, hurt, jaded, or bitter, you'll just live the rest of our life tired, hurt, jaded, or bitter .

God's Word works if you work the Word.

IF YOU DON'T *FIGHT,* THEN YOU DON'T *WIN*

How sad! That's a terrible way to live the only life you'll ever be given. If you're going to win in this race, you've got to pull up your big girl panties or big boy briefs and fight for it. Period.

You are the lead character in the book of your life, and you decide what the narrative is. Yes, there are supporting characters that affect and influence your story, but they do not decide the outcome. There is an expected end in the life of every believer, and that expected end is "We Win." I challenge you, today, that no matter what chapter you are on to make the rest of your story the *best* of your story. Only you decide what your story is about. I absolutely love this quote by Michael Korda:

> Success on any major scale requires you to accept responsibility. . . . In the final analysis, the one quality that all successful people have . . . is the ability to take responsibility.[28]

Take control of your life. Can you control everything that happens in your life? Absolutely not, but you can control the things that you are responsible for. Former first lady Eleanor Roosevelt once said, "In the long run, we shape our lives, and we shape ourselves. The process never ends until we die. And the choices we make are ultimately our own responsibility."[29]

What will you do with the rest of your story?

---

28 Shelby Scarbrough, "I'm Responsible: Eight Steps Every Leader Should Take to Inspire Accountability," *Forbes*, 3 Nov. 2021, www.forbes.com/sites/forbesbooksauthors/2021/11/03/im-responsible-eight-steps-every-leader-should-take-to-inspire-accountability/?sh=533393719906.
29 Erika Andersen, "10 Quotes from the 'First Lady of the World,'" *Forbes*, 10 Jan. 2013, www.forbes.com/sites/erikaandersen/2013/01/10/10-quotes-from-the-first-lady-of-the-world/?sh=4aa73f66272b.

WHAT'S STOPPING YOU?

"There is no failure except in no longer trying."
—ELBERT HUBBARD[30]

"Our greatest weakness lies in giving up. The most certain way to succeed is always to try just one more time."
—THOMAS EDISON[31]

"Not everyone gets to be a winner unless they choose to be. Winning is a mentality."
—VALENTIN CHMERKOVSKIY[32]

---

30 Evelyn Briggs Baldwin, *The Search for the North Pole*, 1896, 520 (public domain).
31 Thomas Edison, Quote in *The St. Albans Daily Messenger*, 2 Jun. 1958.
32 Elizabeth Kwiatkowski, "'Dancing with the Stars' pro Val Chmerkovskiy on Early Exit with Sailor Brinkley-Cook: It Sucks, I Don't Think It's Right," *Reality TV World*, 25 Oct. 2019, www.realitytvworld.com/news/dancing-with-stars-pro-val-chmerkovskiy-on-early-exit-with-sailor-brinkley-cook-it-sucks-i-dont-think-it-right-26658.php.

IF YOU DON'T *FIGHT,* THEN YOU DON'T *WIN*

ooking back over my life, I've been a go-getter since birth. My parents tell the story of the two-year-old Hope who ran down the church aisle into the pastor's arms when he asked, "Does anyone wanted to sing today?" They say I darted off the pew before they could even grab me. I proceeded to hold the microphone and sing a solo—at two years old. I was born with musical talents and obviously wasn't afraid to use them. By the time I was twelve years old, I was going to a different church every weekend to sing for revivals, special services, or just good ole Friday night "singings." Singing came easy for me and I guess that's why it wasn't *hard* or *scary*.

My brother Jody was born with athletic skills. He could pick up any type of ball and play and play well. Me . . . not so much. I had legs up to my chin and they were—emphasis on *were*—as thin as spaghetti noodles. I was long, lanky, and very uncoordinated. I wanted my older brother to be impressed with and proud of me, so I tried out for the junior varsity basketball team during my eighth-grade year. I tried so hard. I was fearful and

IF YOU DON'T *FIGHT,* THEN YOU DON'T *WIN*

insecure every day during practice. I could never do a layup, and dribbling was not something that came naturally to me, especially while trying to run. I'm sure I looked like a drunk giraffe on the court. Needless to say, I didn't make the team. It was quite embarrassing—not only for me but for my brother too. Here's the point I want to make: singing was easy, and ball was difficult, but I tried anyway! How would I ever have known if I could do it if I allowed the fear and insecurities to paralyze me from trying?

When Ron and I married and went into ministry, Ron was the preacher. I had a music degree and played the piano as best I could, sang, and led worship for many years. I did not go to seminary like Ron did. I didn't know how to write sermons or speak hermeneutically. Because we started Redemption as church planters, we had to basically do everything on our own for many years. In addition to leading worship, I taught children's church, typed the bulletins, helped in the office, cleaned the carpets, stacked chairs, led women's nights, answered the phone, and utilized my car as the church taxi. I never thought that I would ever preach or speak, but I had to lead the women's groups, so I started by "sharing." Well one share led to another, and then I started getting asked to come share at other churches.

I was so afraid, mostly because I felt I wasn't qualified to speak. I had no formal training, and I wasn't a Bible scholar. Still, I knew that these open doors were from God and that I was supposed to walk through them, even though I thought I didn't have enough knowledge or enough ability. God knew otherwise, and I knew He was telling me to go. So, I went. Here

I am today, twenty-five years later, traveling all over the world "sharing" (lol) the good news about the wonderful things God has done in and through me. What if I had not stepped out in faith all those years ago? What if I had reasoned myself into believing that I wasn't "qualified," so I must not be called to go?

> **Whether we are working with a little or a lot, it really doesn't matter to God.**

Whether we are working with a little or a lot, it really doesn't matter to God. The things that we think limit us or disqualify us God doesn't consider when He is calling us to do something for Him. Throughout the Bible, God takes the little and turns it into much. The Bible describes many accounts in which God called people to do great things, but they weren't necessarily suitable.

- » God used David's sling and rocks to take down a mighty giant.
- » God asked for the widow's last jar of oil, such a little thing, but turned it into a miracle for her, her son, and the prophet. Her obedience didn't just supply her. Her obedience nourished everyone around her.
- » When God asked Moses to go to Pharoah, Moses responded with "What if they don't believe?" God replied,

IF YOU DON'T *FIGHT,* THEN YOU DON'T *WIN*

"What is that in your hand?" That seems such an odd response to me. That staff in his hand had nothing to do with the assignment. The staff didn't enable him to speak properly or make him more believable. The staff was what he had, and that is all God is asking us to do: use what we have.

» What about the little boy's lunch in John 6:1-14? The multitudes were hungry, and the disciples didn't have enough food to feed them. The five loaves and two fish were not enough, but God still asked for it.

If we will trust God with the little that we have, God will turn it into something powerful. If we were smart enough, gifted enough, cool enough, rich enough, tall enough, athletic enough, or talented enough, we wouldn't need God; therefore, it wouldn't require faith. "And it is impossible to please God without faith. Anyone who wants to come to him must believe that God exists and that he rewards those who sincerely seek him" (Hebrews 11:6, NLT). None of us have what it takes to walk out the amazing plan of God for our lives. That's how He gets the glory. Second Corinthians 12:9 (NLT) concurs:

> [God said to the apostle Paul], "My grace is all you need. My power works best in weakness." So now I am glad to boast about my weaknesses, so that the power of Christ can work through me.

Singing came naturally to me, basketball did not. Did I make the basketball team? No, but I didn't let my lack of ability stop me from trying. I overcame my fear and lack of confidence just by trying. I did it. I didn't make the team, but did I really fail? I don't think so because I overcame a lot of personal issues just by trying. My faith muscle grew stronger that year. I realized that I didn't have to be anything other than who I was created to be. I learned that even if I'm not great at a certain skill, I can at least get a little better just by trying. Just like John Maxwell says: Sometimes you win. Sometimes you learn.[33]

> **If we will trust God with the little that we have, God will turn it into something powerful.**

What if you don't make the team? What if you don't get the date? What if you don't get the promotion? You can "what if" 'til the pigs fly and live a life that never sees the power of God at work in and through you. Faith is taking the first step, even when the lights are off, and you can't see the entire staircase. I believe that courage is rising in you right now to jump into the deep waters where YOU KNOW God is asking you to go—the deep waters of a new job, a new city, a new skill, a new friend group, or even the deep waters of a new commitment to Him.

---

[33] John C. Maxwell, *Sometimes You Win–Sometimes You Learn: Life's Greatest Lessons Are Gained from Our Losses* (New York, NY: Center Street, 2015).

IF YOU DON'T *FIGHT,* THEN YOU DON'T *WIN*

Once you find out the nature and character of God, you will begin to trust Him on a deeper level. He really can be trusted with our lives. He wants more for us than we do, and His route is really the quickest route to finding life and peace. I've birthed three children into this world: Chase, Chaz, and Chanlin. All I've ever wanted was to have children and the Lord blessed me with three of the most amazing children. My pregnancies were easy but when it came to the actual birth . . . that's another story. My first son took thirty-two hours of labor, my second child was eighteen hours, and our last child was twelve hours. Most women have their children within a four-to-eight-hour period; but of course, not me. My water would usually break and then nothing else would happen. Most women go right into labor or labor starts, the water breaks and the baby is in the mother's arms shortly after. Of course, my labor would be completely opposite. Life is very similar to my labor and delivery; God will give you the desire (the baby) and the end result (delivery), but the in-between—the labor—only God knows that process. Remember the Scripture, "'For I know the plans I have for you,' declares the Lord" (Jeremiah 29:11)? Well, that's literally the truth: only God knows the steps it will take for you to *birth that baby*, so to speak. There is a due season for every plan, hope, dream, and purpose in our lives but only God knows the how and when for it to come to pass. Galatians 6:9 (ESV, author emphasis) says, "and let us not grow weary of doing good, for in DUE SEASON we will reap, if we do not give up." There is an appointed time to birth, to hold the dream in our arms, but there are also hundreds of things that will come before that "due season" to tempt you to throw your hands up in frustration and say, "I quit. It's just not worth it."

Joseph's story in the Bible is a perfect example of this process. Joseph had a dream (the end result) of his brothers bowing down to him, but Joseph had no idea that the process, the plan that God would use to bring it about, would be so excruciating. The PLAN, THE PROCESS, would require betrayal, a pit, jail cells, accusations, and years of isolation before the due season of the dream would become a reality. Why do we think that our stories will be different? That is why we are told that fainting or giving up cannot be an option if we hold the reality of our dream in our hands. Oh, the end result is so worth the horrible hours of labor that are required, the sweat drops of blood in the gethsemane stage of the process.

Let me ask you again: What is stopping you? What obstacles have you encountered in your journey that are making you want to faint before you reach the finish line? Is it fear, insecurity, low self-esteem, pride, self-sufficiency, or stubbornness? Let me ask you another question. Are you ready? "HOW IS THAT WORKING FOR YOU?" Remember the illustration I used in chapter 5 about taking your car to the manufacturer? If you're stuck, if you're mad at yourself for where you are in life, and if you're ready to win, then surrender your heart to the Lord right now. He's been waiting patiently, and He's the only One who knows what your life was designed for.

IF YOU DON'T *FIGHT,* THEN YOU DON'T *WIN*

If you're reading this book, I know that you want more out of life than you're currently experiencing. Maybe you're failing, or you're feeling unfulfilled. You want to see more, have more, and be more. What's stopping you? You know the old saying, "If I always do what I've always done, I'll always get what I've always gotten"? Well, it's time to make some changes to get a different result. The biggest change is coming in the realization that you are not the CEO of your life, and the quicker you submit to that, the quicker you will begin to flourish and WIN. Will you reach your potential? Only you will decide.

> **It's time to make some changes to get a different result.**

WE WIN

"You were born to win, but to be a winner, you must plan to win, prepare to win, and expect to win."
—ZIG ZIGLAR[34]

"Success is almost totally dependent upon drive and persistence. The extra energy required to make another effort or try another approach is the secret of winning."
—DENIS WAITLEY[35]

---

34 Zig Ziglar, "You Were Born to Win," *Ziglar Inc*, 28 Mar. 2017, www.ziglar.com/quotes/you-were-born-to-win-but-to-be-a-winner/.
35 Dave Kerpen, "These 17 Quotes Will Inspire You to Be More Persistent," *Inc.*, 6 Nov. 2017, www.inc.com/dave-kerpen/17-quotes-to-inspire-persistence.html.

IF YOU DON'T *FIGHT,* THEN YOU DON'T *WIN*

"Rome wasn't built in a day," is such a simple yet powerful statement, but how does that apply to you and me? Our lives aren't built in a day either. Our lives will be built day by day, month by month, year by year, failure by failure, and victory by victory. We'll experience joy and sorrow, ups and downs, and good days and bad days, until we cross over the finish line and see Jesus face-to-face.

> **Our lives will be built day by day, month by month, year by year, failure by failure, and victory by victory.**

I love this quote by American journalist Hal Borland: "Knowing trees, I understand the meaning of patience. Knowing

IF YOU DON'T *FIGHT,* THEN YOU DON'T *WIN*

grass, I can appreciate persistence."[36] Have you every planted a tree in your yard? Did it grow into an amazing strong, tall, giver of shade overnight? Or have you ever planted grass in your yard? It develops a bit more quickly, and then it seems to multiply and multiply over and over. Our lives must be both: patience and persistent.

No human who has ever lived has gone through life unscathed; pain, sorrow, and loss have been a part of every person's journey. Every life will have moments when we are filled with doubt and fear, our joy will fade to tears, and we'll want to throw our hands up in defeat. It's in those times we must understand that a real walk and relationship with the Lord is a series of mountains and valleys, rain and shine, days when we are giddy in love with our spouse and other days when we could walk out of the front door and never come back. There will be seasons when our prayers are answered quickly and then moments when we question if God is there at all. There will be times we all miss the mark, sin, and fall off the cart, and the shame will be so heavy that we can't look anyone in the eye, and times of regret so heavy that we can't see the light at the end of the tunnel. In these moments, in these dark days, we must remember that we have an enemy who *wants* us to give up, pack our bags, run back to the bottle, entertain the compliments in our direct messages, and declare, "Life's just too hard, so I quit." But if you quit, if you stop fighting the good fight, you won't win. You won't finish the one and only

---
36 Hal Borland, *Countryman: A Summary of Belief* (Philadelphia, PA: Lippincott, 1965) 99.

life you've been given, standing to say, "I finished my course. I ran my race well."

> **The TRUTH of God's Word will always override FACTS.**

The evil days are going to come, sometimes out of the blue, but we must be found standing firm. Standing, knowing who we are in Christ, regardless of our present situation or circumstance. The TRUTH of God's Word will always override FACTS. The fact may be that you are sick in your body, but the truth is, you are already healed by the blood of Jesus (see Isaiah 53:5). The fact may be that you are struggling financially, but the truth is that you are well-supplied (Philippians 4:18), and God supplies all your needs according to His riches in glory. Our God has no needs.

Our righteousness is in Him, so we must daily engage by putting on the breastplate of righteousness that covers a vital organ, the heart. The breastplate is attached to the belt of truth, and if it's not fitted properly, the truth over your situation—the breastplate—will be compromised. If you do not operate out of truth when the enemy starts throwing those darts at you, then your heart won't be strong enough to stand. The truth of God's

IF YOU DON'T *FIGHT,* THEN YOU DON'T *WIN*

Word about you and your situation helps you to know how to react and what to say when all hell is breaking loose against you. GOD'S WORD is what keeps you standing firm. Look at 1 Thessalonians 5:8 (NKJV, emphasis added): "But let us who are of the day be sober, putting on the breastplate of faith and love, and as a helmet of HOPE of salvation."

On the day of trouble, **be sober.** I don't know about you, but there have been times when I wasn't sober. I mean really physically intoxicated, and when you're intoxicated, you don't see or reason clearly. You talk to people you normally wouldn't talk to. That guy you danced all night with at the club . . . you remember him? The one you would've never even given a second glance had you not been intoxicated? Yes, him. You do things you normally wouldn't do. I've seen people vomit in public or urinate in public. Oh, come on, don't act like you've been saved since birth. Even if you haven't done something stupid, I know you've seen other people act crazy. So what this Scripture is saying is this: when trouble hits your life, be sober. Don't lose your mind; don't do things and say things that, in a normal situation, you'd never say or do. Rather, secure that breastplate of right-standing, tighten up that belt of truth, and secure that helmet of hope. IT'S NOT ALWAYS GOING TO BE LIKE THIS. Better days are coming, friend. Sober up, and get yourself together. The enemy comes to get you to doubt the goodness and faithfulness of our God; he says that God just isn't really that good or that faithful.

Do you know how banks train people to tell counterfeit money from real money? They don't keep showing them the counterfeit, having them examine every detail of the fake. No! They make them study the real money so that when a counterfeit shows up, they can tell it immediately. Whew! I hope you're getting this. No matter what the enemy or life, in general, throws our way, the real truth should be so evident to you that you won't fall for the lies of the counterfeit. Stop saying counterfeit statements like, "God won't fix this for me," "This will never work out," "I can't catch a break," "My husband will NEVER change," or "I'll never be able to get ahead." This is counterfeit—contrary to the truth of the Word of God. Check your belt of truth, friend. You will only be able to stand on the truth that you KNOW. BE SOBER. BE WATCHFUL. BE VIGILANT. Becoming skillful with the Word makes life much easier and sweeter. It doesn't mean trouble won't come to visit you, but it does mean that you won't be troubled by it; it won't have the same effect on you.

In this fight of faith, this race, we will have to look at our present situations and say what God says—not what we see, hear, or feel. In your time of need and opposition, tell your need what God says. Look again at Abraham in Romans 4. *You're old Abraham, but you're going to have a child.* Abraham believed it, and it was counted to him as RIGHTEOUSNESS. RIGHT-STANDING. It was probably hard to believe, seeing his present elderly circumstances, but he was sober. He believed what God said. Sarah's womb was as good as dead, but he believed God against all hope. I need to prophesy to you today: if you will believe God—against all hope—it will put you in right standing with God.

IF YOU DON'T *FIGHT,* THEN YOU DON'T *WIN*

Look back over your life; do you not have enough history with God to see that He's been faithful to you all your life? I wish you would remember where you were ten, fifteen, or twenty years ago. God has seen you through things that you swore—then—you'd never get through. Look at you now; you made it. There've been so many times that God showed you mercy when you didn't deserve it, grace when you weren't worthy, and got you out of trouble when you deserved to be UNDER the jail. I'm calling for some sober people today who, when all hell's breaking loose around them—kids acting the fool, husband didn't come home, just got fired, just got an eviction notice, people assassinating your character—you will stay sober! You won't be moved by what you see and hear and feel. Sober up! Clear your thinking. Say what God says over your life.

> **If you've got breath in your lungs, God still has a plan for your life.**

You might be saying, "Hope, I've lost so much. So much time has been taken from me. How can God redeem my story?" Sometimes, you've got to fight for what you've got left. Grieve what's gone, stand up straight, and fight for the days you have left. If you've got breath in your lungs, God still has a plan for your life. If the enemy gets you stuck over what's gone and what's gone wrong, he will keep you from occupying what you have left. Life has a tricky way of making you think you can't make it. Things hit you, and you start to stumble; you start to waiver. But if you can muster up enough strength to get up and run again, put one foot in front of the other; it might not look good, you might have to do it ugly, but do it anyway. It's the only way you'll win.

When you are born again, you are God's child and an heir to everything, but until you rise up and come into maturity, using what belongs to you, you're going to live like every other servant, instead of an heir occupying and obtaining everything that belongs to you. Let's go ahead and put it out there:

1) Crap is going to hit the fan in your life from time to time.
2) There will be enemies assigned to you, on a mission to take you out.
3) God uses trials and tests, on purpose, to grow us, mold us, and shape us.

If you are going to win, you must:

1) Understand pain and trouble are inevitable.
2) Run toward your giant saying what God says.
3) Embrace pain knowing that it produces.
4) Run with endurance with your eyes fixed on Jesus.
5) Grow through what you go through.

I think too many of us live our lives with all our God-given potential just lying dormant on the inside because we refuse to press on and fight for the life that we see in our minds and in our spirits. We've allowed pain, past hurts, and failures to derail us

IF YOU DON'T *FIGHT,* THEN YOU DON'T *WIN*

and hold us captive to a mediocre life that we hate. What if you fail? What if the business doesn't work out? What if you lose the money? Let me ask you this—what if it works? If God has given you a dream, a vision or even a Word, it's not your responsibility to make it happen. It's Gods responsibility to bring it to pass. It's your responsibility to be faithful. Jeremiah 1:12 (NLT, emphasis added) says, "And the Lord said, 'That's right, and it means that I am watching and I WILL certainly carry out all my plans.'" He will carry out the plans for our lives, but we must be willing to get back up again after *every* disappointment, *every* failure, *every* heartbreak and *every* betrayal. We must trust God with our lives and believe that He will carry out His plans for OUR good and HIS glory (Romans 8:28).

I'm believing that today you will rise into the knowledge of who you are in Christ. *You* need to start believing it too. You will only have what you believe is yours, and you won't know what is yours until you seek out the kingdom of God for yourself. Faith is released by what you say and what you do. The more you know the Word and speak the Word, the more you will see it manifest in your situation. The only part of the promises of God that you will walk in and occupy will be the part of the promises that you know and that you stand on. You will not automatically have what's available to you—only the part that you put a demand on. Don't just be a hearer of the Word but be a doer of the Word also (James 1:23).

One of the most important aspects of walking out the promises of God in our lives is this: you don't have to have the big picture to start winning. There's a quote in the book *The Boy, the Mole, the Fox and the Horse* by Charlie Mackesy.[37] The boy and the horse are in the woods, and the boy says to the horse, "I can't see my way through."

The horse replies, "Can you see the next step?"

The boy says, "Yes."

The horse says, "Just take it."

Wow!!!! We aren't promised tomorrow; we only have today. We only have the instruction, the bread, for today, and if we will lean into the instruction for RIGHT NOW and be quick, obedient followers, then we win. We win today. Today is what counts. Then we wake up tomorrow, and we listen and obey. Then we wake up the next day, and we listen and obey. Soon, we look back, see the beauty of how far we've come, all the good things we've accomplished, and how faithful He's been to us on our journey. Will you fall? Will you get frustrated? Will you want to slap three people before lunch somedays? Yes, yes, and yes, but be quick to get back up and keep running with your eyes fixed on Him, Jesus, the author and finisher of your faith—your race. Then . . . my friend . . . you win.

I can say with assurance that God has woven all the tattered, broken, unfaithful pieces of my life TOGETHER with the accomplishments, victories, and beautiful times of my life—and it just seems to make sense. God wants to do the same thing for every one of us, but He needs our cooperation to keep going. Be tired, but get back up. Be mad, but get back up. Question

---

[37] Charlie Mackesy, *The Boy, the Mole, the Fox and the Horse* (New York, NY: HarperOne, 2019).

IF YOU DON'T *FIGHT,* THEN YOU DON'T *WIN*

what you need to question, but decide to trust His faithfulness and goodness in your life. Take a break if you need to, but don't tap out because IF YOU DON'T FIGHT, THEN YOU DON'T WIN.

> **I can say with assurance that God has woven all the tattered, broken, unfaithful pieces of my life TOGETHER with the accomplishments, victories, and beautiful times of my life—and it just seems to make sense.**

FIND HOPE AT

- @PASTORHOPE.CARPENTER
- @PASTORHOPEC
- @PASTORHOPE1
- @HOPECARPENTER

Join Hope in her monthly mentoring group

INNER CIRCLE

CLAIM YOUR FREE BOOK
+
**30-DAY FREE
INNER CIRCLE ACCESS**

CLAIM YOUR *FREE* TRIAL SUBSCRIPTION

AvailJournal.com

To claim your subscription ($29 value)

SCAN HERE TO LEARN MORE

www.ingramcontent.com/pod-product-compliance
Lightning Source LLC
Chambersburg PA
CBHW070543090426
42735CB00013B/3062